The Witches' Almanac

Spring 2014 — Spring 2015

CONTAINING pictorial and explicit delineations of the
magical phases of the Moon together with information about astrological
portents of the year to come and various aspects of occult knowledge
enabling all who read to improve their lives in the old manner.

The Witches' Almanac, Ltd.

Publishers   Providence, Rhode Island
www.TheWitchesAlmanac.com

Address all inquiries and information to
THE WITCHES' ALMANAC, LTD.
P.O. Box 1292
Newport, RI   02840-9998

10-ISBN: 0-9824323-9-9
13-ISBN: 978-0-9824323-9-6

ISSN: 1522-3183

First Printing June 2013

Printed in USA

Printed on recycled paper

Established 1971 by Elizabeth Pepper

Preface

The Witches' Almanac, now in its 33rd edition, has survived Y2K, the birth of Homeland Security, and the end of the Mayan calendar. Our first edition, published in 1971, had a light green cover, contained 90 pages, and was printed in Pine Bush, NY. It sold for $1.00. Since then, our format has changed. We now boast a larger size, heavier stock, staple-less spine, a full color cover, and this year we have expanded to 208 pages.

But to this day, one thing has not changed.

The late Elizabeth Pepper began The Witches' Almanac and, with it, she gave birth to its own personal talisman: The Witches' Almanac's colophon.

Some readers see this symbol as an oval enclosing a bat – control over nature and darkness. Some see a bird flying straight up to the heavens – transcendence from the earthly plane. Others even see mountain peaks through an airplane window – reaching for one's goals. What exactly is this mysterious symbol? Many asked Elizabeth that question and varied answers were returned with a smile. The same answer was almost never given twice. She wanted each reader to see what they needed to see in her design.

I believe that Elizabeth created the colophon from a place of inspiration deep within her own heart. She used this talisman to give birth to The Witches' Almanac and all of its future publications. This is a gift she left us and none of us will ever know exactly what was in her mind when she drew it. I know what she told me, but I'm keeping it a secret!

∞ HOLIDAYS ∞
Spring 2014 to Spring 2015

Art Director . . . . Karen Marks	**ANDREW THEITIC**	
Astrologer . . . . Dikki-Jo Mullen	Executive Editor	
Climatologist . . . . Tom C. Lang	**GREG ESPOSITO**	
Cover Art and Design. . . . Kathryn Sky-Peck	Managing Editor	
Production Consultant . . . . . . Robin Antoni	**JEAN MARIE WALSH**	
Sales . . . . Ellen Lynch	Associate Editor	
Shipping, Bookkeeping . . . . . D. Lamoureux	**JUDIKA ILLES**	
	Copy Editor	

CONTENTS

CONTENTS

Changeling

I am out on the wind
  In the wild, black night;
On the wings of the owl
I take my flight,
On the ghostly wings of the great white owl;
And whether the night be fair or foul,
Or the moon be up or the thunder growl,
Happy I be,
Happy I be
When the changeling blood runs green in me!

When meek folk sleep
In their dull, soft beds,
I creep over roots
That the weasel treads,
Where the squat green lamps of the toadstools glow –
And only the fox knows the ways I go,
And nobody knows the things I know…
Wise I be,
Wise I be
When the changeling blood runs green in me!

O Mother, slumber
And do not wake!…
Thin voices called
From the rain-wet brake,
And the child you cradled against your breast
Is out in the night on the black wind's crest,
For only the wild can give me rest…
Sad I be,
Sad I be
When the changeling blood runs green in me.

– LEAH BODINE DRAKE

Yesterday, Today and Tomorrow

by Timi Chasen

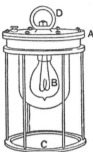

ELECTRIC LADY UP-DATE. Edith, first introduced to our *Almanac* readers in issue #31, continues to endure an adversarial relationship with the electronics in her everyday life. Known for blowing out hundreds of light bulbs and interfering with a range of electronic devices merely by her presence, Edith's peculiar condition presents ever more challenges, as technology progresses and proliferates.

Extended-life light bulbs fail to deliver on their promises. Instead of years, in Edith's presence, most last only a few months and some only a few days. Edith refuses to touch a computer for fear of what could happen. If even small appliances spark as she enters a room, who's to say what would happen to a computer?

Simply being in contact with her daughter has caused her daughter's computer to malfunction. Although her daughter is an experienced computer user, when she tried uploading Edith's picture into Ancestry.com it wouldn't work. It took her daughter many attempts, as well as a software shutdown and full computer reboot, to finally upload a simple photo.

On days when Edith's emotions are particularly elevated, the activity becomes worse. When Edith became frustrated and "lost it" with a contractor, she raised both hands and her voice, causing the entire building's power to suddenly go out, including that of a contiguous business. We wish Edith tranquility and good health, and since Edith cannot use a Kindle, we hope she will read this in a paperback copy of *The Witches' Almanac*!

A FELINE'S TRIBUTE. Toldo, a sleek gray and white tabby from the Italian village of Montagnana, remains devoted to his master, even after his master's death. In the year since Iozzelli Renzo's passing, Toldo has visited his gravesite every day. More remarkable still, Toldo brings gifts to adorn the grave, such as small twigs or leaves and plastic cups.

Ever since the funeral, which Toldo also attended, the cat has been spotted keeping a solitary vigil at the grave or accompanying Renzo's widow on walks to and from the cemetery. The widow believes Toldo is thanking her departed husband for the love he shared with the feline, whom he raised from a kitten.

It is interesting to note that Toldo's first piece of tribute to his departed master, delivered the morning after the funeral, was a sprig of acacia. According to ancient Egyptian lore (which also points to cats as being divine creatures), acacia is associated with the goddess Iusaaset and the Tree of Life, symbolizing death, rebirth, and immortality. Perhaps Toldo is seeking to escort his beloved friend through the afterlife in gratitude for affections garnered in this one.

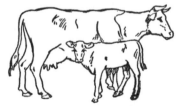

THE OLD WHEYS. Shards of pottery studded with small holes could be the most ancient evidence of cheese making ever uncovered. Excavated in Poland and approximately 7,500 years old, the perforated shards contain traces of animal fats, determined to be from cow's milk. The unique sieve-like pottery was most likely used to strain curds from whey. Necessity may have precipitated the creation of cheese during the Neolithic Age, when the domestication of animals provided the opportunity for harvesting milk.

Dairy is an important source of nutrients, but raw milk spoils quickly. By processing milk into cheese, these pioneering farmers could preserve a vital food source for uncertain times. Turning milk into cheese had the added benefit of greatly reducing the amount of lactose present; something that would be hugely helpful, as most of the population of that time is believed to have been lactose intolerant. Early cheese-makers may have contributed to shaping our evolutionary path. In addition, their prehistoric efforts have since borne tremendous artistic fruits. So next time you are grubbing on gruyere or gorging on gorgonzola, remember to thank our Neolithic ancestors for their ingenuity.

ROYAL MURDER MYSTERY. Modern medical technology offers fresh insight into the death of Ramses III, considered to be Egypt's last great pharaoh. Long believed to be the victim of a coup orchestrated by his wife and son, the exact circumstances of Ramses' death have remained obscure – until now.

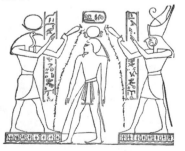

The pharaoh's mummified remains were examined by researchers using CTG scanners, advanced medical equipment usually employed to diagnose the living. Scans revealed a deep laceration across Ramses' throat, one that was almost certainly fatal. The cut was previously hidden by the mummy's dressing, which could not be removed due to preservation concerns.

The scans also revealed an Eye of Horus amulet tucked directly into the throat laceration.

Egyptologists speculate the amulet was placed there by embalmers seeking to heal the wound in the afterlife, as the ancient Egyptians believed the manner in which the body was treated had a direct impact on the deceased's experience of the afterlife. Genetic tests were also performed on the pharaoh's mummy, as well as on an unidentified mummy found near his tomb.

This unidentified mummy – nicknamed "the Screaming Mummy" – was suspected to be Prince Pentawere, the son implicated in Ramses' assassination. Ritualistic 'mishandling' of the remains (organs were not removed and the body was shrouded in impure goatskin) already suggested that the deceased was marked for punishment

in the afterlife. Genetic analysis now confirms that the Screaming Mummy shares fifty percent of its genetic material with Ramses, strongly indicating that he was Ramses' offspring.

ATLANTIS AT LAST?
An image captured by Google Earth, purported to reveal  an underwater grid of city streets off the Moroccan coast, was nothing more than a glitch. The eerie angular artifact caused much excitement, inspiring many to opine that the Lost City of Atlantis may finally have been uncovered. However, the faint traces disappeared with an update to Google mapping technology.

Would-be explorers should not feel too thwarted in their efforts, however. Precedent exists for the discovery of vast, sunken cities, as, for example, the recent discovery of an underwater city in the Gulf of Cambay, off India's western coast. Remains of a large and advanced civilization were discovered, more than one hundred feet beneath the water's surface. Researchers believe this city was lost at the end of the last ice age, when glacial melting caused sea levels to rise, thus inundating the city.

Similar discoveries have been made off the coasts of Cuba and Brazil. Many more coastal sites may lie hidden under turbulent waters, inaccessible to explorers. Perhaps, as imaging technology becomes more and more advanced, we will gain a clearer view of the sea floor and finally catch more than a fleeting glimpse of the Lost City of Atlantis.

THE TEMPLE OF THE NIGHT SUN. Explorers have had better luck uncovering lost civilizations in the jungles of Guatemala, where a Mayan temple has been revealed at El Zotz, once a small, but imposing Maya kingdom and site of the Diablo Pyramid. Archaeologists stumbled upon the temple, while exploring looter's tunnels leading from El Diablo. Archaeologists believe that the temple, which has been dubbed the Temple of the Night Sun for its dramatic engravings of a shape-shifting sun god, was built around 400 CE, as a memorial to the founder of the Pa' Chan or "fortified sky" dynasty. Kingship was strongly associated with the sun god, so it is not at all surprising to see a Mayan monarch honored with depictions of a fearsome sun. Hidden by centuries of overgrowth, the temple imagery is brilliant and somewhat frightening: the sun rises as a thrashing shark, rests at noon to consume blood, and finally descends as a snarling jaguar. Now excavated, tourists may soon be granted a glimpse of the Night Sun.

COME WITH US, IF YOU WANT TO LIVE… Researchers at Cambridge University's Center for the Study of Existential Risk have turned their attentions to the problem of robotic revolution. Founded to examine serious "extinction level" threats to the human race, the Center is now launching an investigation into the possibility that robots will one day surpass their human creators to become the dominant species.

This premise is well known to fans of science fiction, especially the Terminator films. One day, or so the theory goes, a machine will be created that possesses intelligence beyond that of its creator. This machine would be capable of manufacturing yet more hyper-intelligent machines, and so forth, until Earth is overrun with mechanical creatures that can easily outthink their human counterparts. Whether these robotic super beings would use their powers to care for humanity or simply wipe us out is subject to debate.

How serious is the threat posed by these, as of yet, uninvented mechanical killers? Serious enough to merit academic inquiry and to spawn some pretty entertaining movies, as well.

THE EYES HAVE IT

Red strings and baleful glares

"THE EYES are the windows of the soul" is a traditional saying that summarizes the depth and power believed to be contained within a gaze. A quick glance into the eyes of another during the course of a conversation often reveals much more than mere words alone will ever convey. In the United States, the ability to be forthright and look someone in the eye is thought to be indicative of candor, while, in other parts of the world, a direct gaze is perceived as rude and even threatening. Those who are familiar with animal behavior know that direct eye contact may be perceived as a challenge and can elicit either attack or flight.

Over the ages, many have feared that an adversary's "evil eye" – manifested through a jealous glance or angry glare – can cause actual harm to the target. Popular idioms, such as "if looks could kill," "an icy stare" or "a murderous glare" reinforce this belief.

Ancient eyes

Archeologically unearthed artifacts from the upper Paleolithic era indicate that the eye and its powers were a theme in magic and talismans embraced by our cave dwelling ancestors. More recently – about 5000 years ago – cuneiform clay tablets displaying eye motifs appeared in Mesopotamia. Artistic renditions of eyes figure prominently in Jewish, Christian, Muslim, Hindu, and Buddhist spiritual art.

Today, a popular method of repelling the evil eye involves carrying or wearing beautiful glass amuletic eyes, popularly known as "evil eye beads." These glass creations, easily found in metaphysical and import shops, are offered in many sizes and colors. Some are worn as jewelry, while others are intended to be placed in the home, automobile, or work place. The tradition appeared in Anatolia, home of early master-glass craftsmanship, at least three-thousand years ago. These magically protective eyes are known as *nazar boncugu* in Turkish.

Seven knots of safety

Other methods of fending off the evil eye exist,

and not all involve an ocular shape. Those who practice the mystical Kabbalah often employ a red string, another, more subtle defense against the evil eye. Rather than a glass eye, this involves a length of red yarn or cotton string tied on the left wrist with seven knots. Kabbalistic teachings meticulously describe the mechanics of the evil eye and offer remedies and solutions. It is believed that envy or other negative thoughts directed at another by means of a glance can devour the light of the recipient's life force.

Negative forces are believed to bombard and be absorbed into the body from its left side. When worn on the left wrist, the red string deflects this energy. According to the Zohar, among the primary Kabbalistic texts, white wool embodies mercy. In the process of dying white wool red, the colors combine, marrying mercy with judgment. This assures justice for the innocent and protection from the evil eye. The seven knots relate to the seven spiritual worlds, the colors of the rainbow and the chakras. Likewise, Feng Shui practitioners often begin consultations by tying a red ribbon around a client's left wrist, for the purpose of encouraging chi – the universal energy flow – to move in a positive direction.

Before wearing a red string or selecting an evil eye bead, it is always advisable to take a moment to focus your intent.

– ESTHER ELAYNE

A Witch's Garden

Planting herbs

AN OUTDOOR herb garden begins indoors, and your first gardening tools are pencil and paper. Planning at the very beginning will save you many problems later. Decide what specific herbs you really want and how large a garden they will require. As a general rule of green thumb, you can allow a circle with a radius of one foot around each plant. Some herbs require less and some more, but this is a convenient working average.

At this stage you will want to consider just how large a garden will be practical to handle. It is better to start out a bit on the small side; you can always expand gradually. Many novices tackle too much and later find that they have more than they can handle.

The most important step in planning the herb garden is choosing the site. The gardener must be concerned with two extremely important points, sunlight and soil. Most herbs require a great deal of direct sunlight, and starting an herb garden in a spot that is shaded half the day is courting disaster. If you

live in the South or Southwest, where the sunlight is intense, you might get away with this kind of site. Otherwise don't plant in such an area unless you want to limit yourself to the shade-loving herbs such as the mints, sweet cicely, woodruff and similar plants.

Most herbs also require a relatively light, limey, nourishing soil. If your soil is sandy, dig in some humus and possibly add some lime. Dolomite, an excellent form of lime, is relatively easy to handle. Eggshells and ground clam and oyster shells are less effective but of some value. With the heavy clay soil common along the Eastern Seaboard and in parts of the Midwest, you will have to take more serious steps. If your site is well drained or on relatively high ground where drainage can be arranged, dig it up to a depth of two or three feet. Remove about half the spaded-up clay and replace it with a mixture of peat, builder's sand, and compost or humus. Gardeners near the seacoast have learned that seaweed is an excellent conditioner for heavy clay soils. Large

quantities should be dug in, ideally in the autumn so that the winter frosts can "work" the soil mixture. Seaweed that is well rinsed can be dug in during the spring about a month before planting begins.

If the soil is acid or if you have spaded in a large quantity of peat, you will want to add lime in some form. Wood ash and some well-rotted manure will also help. Horse manure is better than cow manure, and rabbit manure is very good. Remember that any type of manure must be well rotted before it is dug into the garden.

Drainage is an important factor. If your site is not well drained, there is little point in digging it up because a heavy rain will turn the garden into a huge mud puddle. Any gardener with a drainage problem would be wise to revive a medieval custom and raise the level of plant beds anywhere from a

foot to two-and-a-half feet. In the Middle Ages the retaining walls of these beds were made of turf or wicker-work, and if you live in a damp climate you might consider turf. In a moist climate or with regular watering, the turf wall becomes attractively green and grassy — and turf is much cheaper than brick. However,

you will have to clip the grass from time to time. If you prefer to use wood, brick or stone, make certain that the foundation of your walls goes below the frost line and that the walls contain numerous small drainage vents.

While your garden is still in the planning stages, work out groups of any plants with special needs. Decide where to put plants such as rosemary, thyme, and lavender, which require a somewhat sandy well-limed soil and a great deal of sun and air, and decide where to put the more acid and shade-loving plants such as woodruff and angelica. It is best to isolate the mints (especially spearmint) as they tend to spread rapidly and drown out their neighbors. Remember to plant the shorter varieties in front of the bed and the taller herbs such as fennel, vervain, dill, and comfrey in back.

In ancient times it was customary to make an offering and invoke the blessing of the Earth Mother when a garden was begun, and some traditionalists as well as many witches keep up this custom. The offering and invocations can take many different forms.

In some parts of the world the gardener walked around the spaded-up garden three times sunwise in a circle chanting a blessing, sometimes twirling a blazing torch, sometimes sprinkling water on the garden. When the first spadeful of earth was dug — or

after the garden had been prepared but before the seeds or herbs were planted – an oatcake, cheese, and a glass of wine or ale were given to Earth Mother in some special part of the garden. Another tradition, which probably goes back to the Neolithic period, calls for a libation of milk and an offering of honeycomb. And in Scotland and Ireland, three days before the seeds were sown they were sprinkled with cold, clear spring water in the name of the gods by a person walking sunwise three times around the seeds. This was usually done on a Wednesday; the seeds were planted on a Friday, the day most auspicious for all operations not requiring the use of iron.

The contemporary herb gardener will probably prefer the modern method of planting the seeds indoors in a sterile medium such as sphagnum moss and setting them out later to avoid "damp-off" and other hazards. But there is no reason that some of the old traditions could not be adapted to the sowing or the transplanting.

Once your garden is established and you have a regular schedule of watering and weeding, you should have few problems unless you are afflicted with rabbits, slugs, earwigs, or other pests. The only answer to rabbits, I fear, is a fence. Toads usually will eat the slugs, and earwigs can be attracted under inverted flower posts during the day and then disposed of. Aphids may attack your basil and mint, but these pests are easily controlled by a number of organic sprays. Basil and nasturtiums are the most likely plants to be attacked by insects, and some people plant rows of nasturtiums to attract insects away from other plants. Most herbs are fairly tough, given the proper growth conditions in the first place.

If you live in a cold climate, cover your garden in winter with a thick mulch after the first frost and leave it until spring definitely has arrived. This will protect the plants from the dry, freezing winds of February and March, which can be fatal to the more tender herbs. From this point on, everything should be smooth sailing.

The Dog in the Manger

ONCE, when the oxen on a farm were returning to their stable tired and hungry after a hard day's work, they found a nasty barking dog standing in the manger where their hay was kept. The dog couldn't eat the hay himself, but he wouldn't allow the hungry oxen to get it, either.

Moral: Don't be a "dog in the manger." If you have something that you don't need and you know that someone else really needs it, don't keep it just for spite.

The Night-Time Mind of the Witch

WHEN MEANDERING in the pages of old folklore that tells of witches, faeries, goblins, and ghosts, it is often striking how rich and vivid these otherworldly events seem to have been for our ancestors. They speak about corpse-candles and hellhounds as though they were as tangible as the milkman. Certainly it didn't hurt that belief in the supernatural was seldom questioned in the pre-modern world. To have no part of the mind constantly fact-checking and sorting, relegating experiences and scrutinizing them for whether they are 'true' or whether you are still sane would certainly have made for a different way of seeing.

Today, in a world of electric lights and other brightly lit forms of entertainment, our senses are regularly overwhelmed well into the late hours once meant for dreaming and storytelling. Not only are most of us brought up to be deeply skeptical of spiritual phenomenon, but we barely get time to enter the twilight states that best open the gates to such moments of sublimity.

First and second sleep

Some modern research into historical sleep patterns suggests that prior to modern streetlights and the greater affordability of candles, sleep occurred differently than today. Not only were more hours spent in darkness, but sleep was 'segmented' into two portions, with a period of prayer, sex, or reading in the middle.

Figures as diverse as Virgil and Nathaniel Hawthorne – separated by the best part of two millennia – both mention the 'first and second sleep.' The Tiv, an indigenous people of central Nigeria, also speak of "first sleep" and "second sleep". They wake at any time during the night and will talk to anyone else who is awake about their dreams. This practice not only emphasizes the value of dreams, but also aids in remembering them.

Lucid dreams and visions

As most lucid dreams and what could be called visions occur during sleep that lasts for no longer than four hours at a time, these differences are truly significant. Research by Dr. Thomas Wehr, chief of the clinical psychobiology branch of the National Institutes of Health, has shown that, when deprived of artificial lighting for several weeks, the average person develops

a very specific sleep pattern: first lying awake in bed for an hour or two, followed by four hours of sleep. This is, in turn, followed by two to three hours of "non-anxious wakefulness." This period is then followed by a second sleep, before the person wakes for the day's activities. All told, these results indicate a considerable amount of time spent in darkness and quiet, where the mind is allowed to tune in to the subtler realm.

If we consider the differences of behavior between the modern day and even a few centuries ago, a backdrop is set, against which one can consider old reports of the supernatural and stories of witchcraft. Prior to the advent  of artificial lighting, there must have been a deeply vivid and still space for shadows to dance and dreams to take on full-blooded, richly textured reality.

Seeking visions from the dark

The "night watch" significantly affects the mind. The interval between first sleep and second sleep is characterized by elevated levels of prolactin, a pituitary hormone best known for helping hens to brood contentedly above their eggs for long periods. Wehr concluded that this liminal state between sleep and wakefulness can produce states of altered consciousness not unlike meditation or trance.

So, for many of us pursuing magical work, knocking on the door of the Otherworld and hoping for an answer – or perhaps increasingly strong responses – there is something to be said for darkness and for cocooning ourselves away from the electric lights and other stimulation that so radically alters our natural dreaming process.

Mental entertainment

Of course, today's life-style can rarely be easily modified to accommodate pre-modern sleep patterns. Although some may be willing, most people will find this too disruptive, including even dedicated occultists. However, it can be very beneficial to selectively engage in periods of darkness, especially when leading up to a major ritual or trance-working.

This can be undertaken during holidays, so as not to disrupt work life. Even if candles are used, if no electrical lights are turned on after dusk, one quickly and naturally becomes tired more rapidly than when stimulated by light. Retiring at the time of tiredness and then sleeping until awakening naturally at some point in the night, at which point one can record dreams and visions, meditate and wait to fall asleep again, can be extremely productive. Instead of watching television in the evening, the mind begins to produce ever more vivid 'entertainment' of its own.

Following the downward tide

These kind of 'light fasts' where electrical light and entertainment is voluntarily given up for a period can be fruitful, even if only done for one night each week. You can take the concept of Earth Hour outside the hour and save resources, whilst also doing something beneficial for your magical life. But all of this will be so much more powerful if you tune your efforts to coincide with other natural cycles.

Wintertime can be a particularly potent time to engage in a night watch of this kind, especially if you live in a region where there are marked differences of day and night lengths around the solstices. You might like, perhaps, to select some nights that have meaning for your particular tradition of witchcraft. For instance, you might like to select nights around Samhain or the winter solstice. However, I would particularly suggest a vigil leading up to the solstice night, concluding with the darkest and longest night of the year.

Spending your evenings with no other light but a hearth fire and your only entertainment being conversation with others or the work of your own hands is a wonderful way to prepare the mind for the deep, liminal winter sleep. Then, when retiring to bed, quietly set your intention to dedicate a chosen number of nights to the darkness vigil and to exploring the twilight states of trance and vision.

As you begin to shut down your electric lights, turning off whatever flashes or beeps, as well as telephones or other potentially disturbing appliances, visualize yourself turning inward, descending widdershins down a spiral staircase. Throughout the night, every time you think about this staircase, take a moment to see yourself walking down a few more stairs.

Going deeper

Anyone who has ever sat around a winter's fire and listened to a good storyteller knows how hypnotic the experience can be. Unlike visual entertainment that shapes a vision for us and demands our focus and waking attention, aural storytelling encourages us to form pictures in our own heads and dream.

This has become so uncommon today that it has been suggested that many children now lack the capacity to listen when they are not also being visually stimulated. Yet it is these active imaginal functions that are so crucial to us as a species. It is these very functions that allow the daydream, as well as the virid mesmerism that is achieved in green places allowing us to sense the spirits of the woodland, of the trees and rocks, and to give them personhood and value. We need to first clear a space before such experiences can fully take root. We need to prepare dark, fertile soil for this "greening" of the mind.

An exercise

If you haven't done so before, take turns at telling a story off the top of your head with a companion. If you feel you can, attempt to imagine a story that emerges out of the land around you. Don't try to control it, just go with it. Allow a story that explains a natural feature or how the ghost on the bridge got to be there or simply a story about what and who dwells within the mountain, nearby cave, ancient tree, or in the river. Children very naturally see stories in their environment, if their imaginations have been allowed to develop in this way. As witches, we should seek to recapture this capacity and gift others with it.

Other ancestral behaviors that can be utilized to entrance and re-enchant ourselves and our world include repetitive tasks undertaken in a state of mindfulness. Hold a rosary or other beaded necklace during your long, dark vigil, passing the beads through your fingers. While seated beside the fire at night,

our ancestors also engaged in knitting and spinning, which can potentially cause altered states of consciousness, if maintained in a quiet state.

If you are planning to attempt to open the way for a deep trance or lucid dreaming episode, you might like to try meditative walking before retiring. Trace a spiral or labyrinth on the floor in chalk and then proceed to walk to its center. The trick is that you must walk as slowly as humanly possible, without stopping. You will discover that, in order to maintain this kind of slow movement, you will need to stay mindful! Simultaneously, remind yourself that, just as your body is now spiraling slowly down into the darkness of all possibility, just so your spirit will journey into the heart of things and return with precious fragments of truth.

– Lee Morgan

Scottish Fishing Magic and the Lore of Boats

BOATS should be *sained* (purified) on one of the great Fire Festivals such as Samhuinn (Halloween), Oimelc (Imbolc, Brighid), Bealltan (May Day), or Lúnasdal (Lammas). Sprinkle salt water upon the vessel and carry a lighted torch around it three times to ward off bad luck. Fishing nets should be sprinkled with whisky and held over a ritual fire to be sained by the smoke. No stranger should ever walk over the fishing tackle and if they do so they must re-trace their steps to undo the harm.

When building a boat, tie a red thread around the first nail for luck and hide a gold coin beneath the mast. A horseshoe should be nailed to the mast for luck. A woman should apply the first mop of tar and, before launching, barley should be sprinkled on the deck for luck and a bottle of spirits broken across the bow. It is very unlucky if a ship has to return to shore after being launched.

Golden earrings, red flannel cloth

Ships made of oak will be fastest in the water and only new wood should be used in boat construction. Examine the knots in the wood: "windy knots" or knots that look like swirling water attract storms, while "fishy knots" or knots that look like fish will attract fish by sympathetic magic.

According to Scottish tradition, carrying a child's caul or golden earrings will protect against drowning. A lump of coal or a cowrie shell are said to bring luck and protection on a voyage. It is also helpful to wear or carry a red flannel cloth – you can also wrap the cloth around your neck if you get a sore throat.

Once on board, a sailor should never mention the place they are headed by its real name, lest the Spirits hear him and cause mischief. No one should call out to the boat from shore once it has launched.

Forbidden words

Fishing boats should move in three *deiseil* (sunwise, clockwise) circles before setting out. Seeing a raven, curlew, or a stormy petrel is a bad omen on leaving shore, as is the sight of geese flying back to land. The sight of swallows or wild geese setting out to sea means good weather.

Never say the following words on board; kirk (church), salt, minister, priest, pig, rabbit, hare, fox, or rat. If any of these words are spoken, you must touch iron to undo the bad luck. If you accidentally spill salt, you must throw some over your left shoulder.

Silvering the water

On shore and also on board, be careful to crush any egg shells, so a sorcerer can't use them to raise a storm. Whistling can also raise a storm, but if a ship is becalmed whistling can help raise a wind. Stick a steel bladed knife into the mast in the direction from which you need the wind.

Wives must never do laundry while their mate is at sea, lest he be washed away by sympathetic magic. To calm an angry sea, "silver the water" by offering silver coins or jewelry to the waves and then wave your hand softly in the opposite direction of the swells.

Lucky black cats

Never allow a cat to touch the bait or fishing gear because the fish will smell the cat and stay away. Black cats are very lucky for sailors, on a ship or on land. Cats can start storms at will and if they lick their fur against the grain it means a hail storm is approaching. If a cat sneezes, it means rain and if a cat is suddenly frisky, it means that the wind will soon pick up.

Never call out to a fisherman as he leaves the house. Ideally he should leave unseen so jealous Spirits won't notice. Placing a bit of grain into the fishing basket attracts luck. On the way to the ship, the fisherman or woman should pick up a stone and say "May I come safely back to where this came from."

Fish while hungry

A fisherman must never throw fish bones into a fire or fish on a full stomach. Fishing while hungry encourages the fish to bite, by sympathetic magic.

Fish will bite more readily at the incoming tide and the first fish caught should always be thrown back, as an offering to the sea.

Fishing lines should be cast and fish hauled in from the starboard side. If the fish are cleaned on deck, the deck must not be swabbed or the good luck might run off. Let the sea birds and weather clean the boat. Fishing is best when the wind is east south east or south south east.

Sea burials

If a fisherman returns with a poor catch, his wife should scold him and kick the bag in which the fish were carried, to drive out the bad luck. At the end of the fishing season, free smoked fish should be shared with widows, orphans, and neighbors.

If a person dies at sea, they should be buried in a canvas bag. If a person drowns, they belong to the sea and should be buried on the 'Black Shore'– the space between the line of seaweed on the beach and the water, so as not to offend the ocean spirits. It is said that an old fisherman will stay alive, as long as his old boat stays mended and whole.

At Samhuinn (Halloween), offerings of ale and oatmeal should be made to the Gods of the Sea. Walk into the water, make your offering and say, "Shony, I give you this cup of ale hoping you will be so kind as to send us plenty of seaweed for enriching our ground in the coming year." Add other requests as needed.

– ELLEN EVERT HOPMAN
from Scottish Herbs and Fairy Lore

A Merry Journey

The game of carousel

THE mention of carousels and merry-go-rounds typically suggests carnival music, cotton candy, and childhood exuberance. However, this appealing ride to nowhere and back again, astride a brightly painted wooden horse, possesses a history that is rich in complexities and subtle magic. Films and stories offer us clues.

For example, the plot of *Something Wicked This Way Comes*, a movie based on the Ray Bradbury story of the same name, pivots around a sinister carousel ride. Riders grow older or younger, depending upon the carousel's direction. Unbelievable consequences ensue. The dramatic climax of Alfred Hitchcock's *Strangers on a Train* occurs as the film's hero and villain struggle on a carousel. In *Mary Poppins*, Mary, Bert, and the Banks children climb aboard a carousel, only for their horses to jump off and take them on an unexpected fox hunt. Warner Brothers Studios used *The Carousel Broke Down*, a novelty song from the 1930s, as the theme music for their Looney Tunes cartoon series.

Little battle and flying horses

The word "carousel" derives from the Spanish or Italian words, *carosella* or *garosello*, which may be translated as "little battle." The earliest known carousel appears on a Byzantine bas-relief, dating from approximately 500 CE, that portrays riders suspended in baskets that moved when a central pole was turned. During the Crusades, an early device was perfected, intended to help horsemen train for combat. Turkish and Arabian soldiers would ride in a circle, making a game of slashing at mock enemies with swords. Travelers from Europe saw this and were impressed.

The concept was transported to Europe, where a ring was added to the contraption, so that it could be speared by the most skillful. Wooden horses replaced baskets for the riders. Carousels gradually replaced real horses during jousting tournaments. Riders could display their courage and agility, without tiring or endangering their mounts. Eventually, music and torches were added to provide after-dark entertainment and the invention was nicknamed "flying horses."

Swaying bears, giraffes, and sea serpents

Eventually, a platform was added to what had previously been just baskets or wooden horses suspended around a pole. Peter Munday, an English traveler, described seeing this predecessor to the modern carousel on a trip to Bulgaria in 1620. By the early 18th century, carousels appeared at fairs and markets across Europe. Swaying chariots, bears, lions, pigs, sea serpents, zebras, giraffes, and other animals joined horses for the ride.

The tradition of English carousel-crafting reflected the Industrial Revolution. At the 1861 New Year Fair in Bolton, Lancashire, an inventor named Thomas Hurst presented the first steam driven example, featuring bevel gears and offset cranks. As a result, fairgoers of all ages were enchanted by music from a steam powered organ, as well as the up-and-down motion of the horses. Both music and vertical motion immediately evolved into the carousel ride's signature characteristics. Merry-go-round, another name for a carousel, was coined in England at about this time.

Carousels come to America

During the 19th century, Old World craftsmen arrived in the United States, where they began to build carousels featuring fine carving and exquisitely painted designs. Excellent wood for carving, such as pine, basswood and poplar, was found in Appalachia. Americans were enchanted.

In 1871, the first patent for a carousel was granted to William Schneider of Davenport, Iowa. Other centers of carousel building were in Philadelphia, New York, Illinois, and Kansas, each taking pride in the durability and beauty of their products. Coney Island, America's premier amusement park opened its first merry-go-round in 1876.

Golden age of the carousel

Dedicated collectors and connoisseurs consider the early 20th century to be the carousel's Golden Age. Electricity and gasoline powered elaborate machines with double decks, flashing lights, and flower-shaped platforms for life-like animals complete with tossing heads, manes of real hair, and glass-jewel accents.

The Great Depression and World War II dealt the carousel industry a death blow. Nearly all carousels fell rapidly into ruin and disuse. Today, carousels are rare treasures, but a few precious jewels survive. It remains possible for dreamers and seekers to discover them and enjoy a spin, while cherishing a tradition of pageantry and beauty dating back to before the Middle Ages.

Riverside, Rhode Island, for instance, offers the Crescent Park Looff Carousel. Newly renovated, it remains in its original 1895 location and features sixty-one horses, a camel, and four chariots. The Arkansas Carousel in Little Rock is the only surviving example of a wooden platform to move in a wave rhythm. Disneyland in Anaheim, California offers the King Arthur Carousel. Built in 1932, it was moved to the theme park for its 1954 opening.

Perhaps the most heartfelt merry-go-round story involves the current World Capital of the Carousel in Binghamton, New York. Its six original carousels were donated by George F. Johnson, the wealthy owner of the Endicott-Johnson Company, with a stipulation. No one is ever to be charged to ride. As a child, Johnson's heart was broken, because he was always too poor to purchase a ticket.

– MARINA BRYONY

The Power of Hair

TALES of infinite strength and secret vulnerabilities didn't begin with Superman. In the biblical story of Samson and Delilah, God granted Samson supernatural strength in order to combat his enemies and perform heroic feats. Among the conditions of this gift, however, was that Samson was not to cut or shave his hair. Samson is tricked into revealing this secret by the temptress Delilah, who then ordered her servant to cut off Samson's hair while he slept. He loses his strength and the Philistines capture and blind him. Only when his hair grows back does he regain his strength and destroy his enemies.

But this is not the only such legend. Many cultures throughout the ages have associated hair with strength and power. Lustrous hair, whether on a woman or man, has historically been linked to fertility, an association that continues today. Healthy hair indicates a healthy body, which improves one's chances of being fertile. Hair that is both lustrous and long indicates not just recent health, but health over the years that it has been growing. In Norse mythology, the grain goddess Sif, renowned for her long, golden tresses, is also a goddess of fertility.

Another connection between hair and strength may be related to the magical doctrine of association or the Contact of Contagion, as Sir James Frazer called it in his opus, *The Golden Bough*. As he wrote, this type of magic is based on the principle that things that have once been in contact "continue ever afterwards to act on each other."

We see this in practice in spells that call for pieces of clothing, fingernail clippings, or, yes, hair, from the person you seek to influence. Should someone's hair be found – or stolen – by an enemy, the enemy can use that hair to gain control over the person. A knowledgeable practitioner could add the hair to a poppet, place it in a charm bag, or weave it into a bracelet or belt. Speaking an incantation or two over the purloined hair could further sap the energy and health of the original owner.

In times past, the careful person would remove stray hairs from brushes and clothing in order to prevent them from falling into the wrong hands. Men, after shaving, would take care to rinse the basin clean. Women might not shave at all, for many consider body hair, especially in the armpits and pubic area, to be erotic. This belief might not have been far off the mark. Among the theories for why humans even possess pubic hair is that it traps sex pheromones – chemicals released by the body to attract sexual partners. In other words, body hair, especially pubic hair, exerts a strength all its own.

Think about that the next time you consider a full bikini wax...

– MORVEN WESTFIELD

Ijermes the Thrice-Greatest

THE WORD "HERMETIC" pops up with some regularity in the occult world, typically in reference to High Magic. It derives primarily from a series of ancient writings known as the *Corpus Hermeticum*, which are attributed to a mysterious author called Hermes Trismegistus, or Hermes the "Thrice-Greatest."

People during the Renaissance believed very strongly that ancient times were far preferable to their current world state. A myth had been propagated, even back during the earliest centuries of the Common Era, that the yonder halcyon days of yore were wondrous times indeed and that the world had degenerated considerably, both intellectually and morally, since then.

"The men of the second century were thoroughly imbued with the idea (which the Renaissance imbibed from them) that what is old is pure and holy, that the earliest thinkers walked more closely with the gods than the busy rationalists, their successors. Hence the strong revival of Pythagoreanism in this age." – Frances A. Yates, *Giordano Bruno and the Hermetic Tradition*. Such an antiquated myth was pushed even further by those of the Renaissance who avidly read the Bible, which claimed astonishingly long life spans for its ancient patriarchs, especially those only a few generations away from Adam.

Ficino and Medici

Egypt held as much of an air of mystery and antiquity during the Renaissance as it does now. Perhaps even more so, as hieroglyphs had yet to be deciphered. What little the learned folk of the Renaissance knew about ancient Egypt had most probably been gleaned from the writings of Plato, Plutarch, and the Old Testament. This changed, however, when the writings of what they believed to be ancient Egyptians fell into the lap of a certain Florentine man fluent in Greek by the name of Marsilio Ficino.

Sometime around 1460 an agent of Cosimo de Medici, a monk by trade or so the stories go, brought a collection of manuscripts back with him from Macedonia that he had acquired for the wealthy patriarch. This collection contained fourteen of the fifteen books deemed to be the *Corpus Hermeticum* – the supposed writings of the mysterious Hermes Trismegistus. Cosimo de Medici had already hired Ficino to translate the scores of Greek manuscripts, including the works of Plato and Plotinus, collected by the Medici family. Medici ordered Ficino to cease translating these other manuscripts, so that he could dedicate all of his time and energy towards deciphering these Hermetic treatises.

It is thought that Medici knew he was near the end of his life and wanted to read the treatises before he died. Ficino finished the translation within a few months. The resulting work ignited a philosophical fire in the minds of many Renaissance thinkers, occult-oriented or otherwise.

Hermes Trismegistus

It should be noted that the writings of Hermes Trismegistus, or at least legends of them, had already spread through Renaissance Europe through two rather unlikely sources: early Christian Church fathers, Lactantius and Augustine had written about Hermes in the third and fourth centuries CE, respectively. Their Latin treatises had been well-circulated and well-read by the time of the Renaissance. In fact, the writings of both of these Christians propagated the myth that Hermes Trismegistus was not only one specific person, but from an ancient, forgotten past. Lactantius, who occasionally quotes sections of the *Corpus Hermeticum*, claims, in his *De ira Dei*, that Hermes is considerably more ancient than both Plato and Pythagoras. Augustine even places him shortly after the time of Moses.

Unlike Augustine, who seemed rather blatantly critical of virtually everything that was not Christian, Lactantius quoted generously from certain Pagan philosophical texts in order to support what he deemed the wisdom of the Christian religion: the writings of the Thrice-Greatest were chock full of references that could very easily be interpreted as "Christian" in nature.

The logos

For instance, Hermes, who somewhat commonly refers to the God of Creation as "Father", also refers to the Demiurge as the "Son of God". In the Hermetic text, *Pimander*, it is said that the act of creation occurs through the power of a luminous Word, the Logos, similar to the *Gospel of St. John*. Lactantius places his blessing upon the writings of the *Corpus Hermeticum* as works inspired by God, but preceding the coming of Christ. "Indeed, Lactantius regards Hermes Trismegistus as one of the most important of the Gentile seers and prophets who foresaw the coming of Christianity, because he spoke of the Son of God and the Word. In three passages of the *Institutes* he cites Trismegistus with the Sibyls as testifying to the coming of Christ. Lactantius nowhere says anything against Hermes Trismegistus. He is always the most ancient and all-wise writer, the tenor of whose works is agreeable to Christianity and whose mention of God the Son places him with the Sibyls as a Gentile prophet." – Frances A. Yates, *Giordano Bruno and the Hermetic Tradition*

Hermetic magical philosophy

This favorable light shed upon the writings of Hermes would spark and inspire the Renaissance occultists to embrace what would from then on be considered Hermetic magical philosophy. As an added bonus, they could do so without fear of either divine or ecclesiastical retribution, as a well-respected and prolific member of the early Church had sanctioned the study of what might, under different circumstances, be considered blasphemous texts.

So seemingly compatible were the writings of Trismegistus to the Renaissance Christians, and so revered by the Church father Lactantius and contemporary scholars alike, that the unthinkable happened: a Pagan image was engraved upon Holy Ground within Siena's cathedral itself.

"In the middle of the pavement one finds a representation of Hermes portrayed as a huge old man with a long beard, dressed in a flowing robe. Under his feet is found the inscription: *Hermes Mercurius Trismegustus Contemporaneous Moysi*. With his right hand, he extends to a deferential wise man an open book with the words: *Suscipite O Licteras et Leges Egiptii* – 'Support thy letters and laws, O Egyptians' – Peter J. French, *John Dee: The World of an Elizabethan Magus*

Holy word

Also included in the representation are the images of a man dressed in Renaissance garb witnessing the event, as well as a table set upon two sphinxes which holds an abbreviated and somewhat modified passage from the Latin version of the *Asclepius*, which roughly translates to "God, the Creator of all things, made the second visible god and made him first and alone, [the second god], in whom He was well pleased, He loved deeply as [he was] His own son, who is called Holy Word." – Peter J. French, *John Dee*. This was done specifically to show that Hermes was actually a prophet of the coming of Christ, as opposed to a mere heathen mystic.

Hermetic fever had spread throughout all of Christendom. Ficino's translations were instant hits. By the 16th century, hundreds upon hundreds of the Renaissance's leading intelligentsia owned copies of the *Corpus Hermeticum* and related works. These were not limited to occultists such as Ficino, Pico Della Mirandola, or

Giordano Bruno. King Phillip II of Spain, Sir Walter Raleigh, and theologian Philippe Du Plessis-Mornay also owned and wrote about the many Hermetic treatises then being disseminated throughout all of Europe.

Birth of the hermetic texts

Though the myth was that the Hermetic treatises were written by a single enlightened master during the era of the biblical patriarchs, in truth, they appear to have postdated not only Pythagoras and Plato, but Christ as well. Scholars date their composition sometime between 100 and 300 CE, during the Roman occupation of Egypt.

Their authors were most probably Greek-speaking Egyptians of various philosophical backgrounds, following a relatively Platonic format. Willis Barnstone, discussing the Hermetic book, *Poimandres*, explains: "Although the author (or authors) of the *Poimandres* is aware of Judaism and Christianity, this syncretic work is basically Pagan, deriving from Egyptian Hellenistic Platonism. False attribution in order to lend authority to a text was a common practice in antiquity – we have many poems incorrectly attributed to Sappho, Plato, Anacreon, and Theognis – as it also was among European bookprinters until very recently. As for religious texts, the practice was the rule." – Willis Barnstone, *The Other Bible*

– ANTHONY TETH

The Emerald Tablet

Heinrich Khunrath, 1606

THE MAGIC OF CAMPING

THERE are few ambivalent responses when the word "camping" is invoked. Most people will either jump up and down enthusiastically or raise their hands in a defiant "over my dead body" posture. It may seem surprising that these two opposing reactions are also prevalent within the general Pagan community. The irony, of course, being that it is generally assumed that most Pagans enjoy quality time with Mother Nature.

Right?

Well, yeah, sure – provided certain conditions are met. The weather is warm, but not too hot. A little damp is okay, especially in a "gentle-sun-showery-oh-look-at-that-rainbow" way. But if it is raining hard enough to get one's hair wet, this is definitely not cool. The length of time one plans to actually spend outdoors is also a factor. Even the least nature loving types will happily commit to a few hours of well-planned seasonal celebration in a greening field, provided that their clothing stays dry and that they can find their way back to the parking lot before dark.

Finding the divine

Overnight camping, however, is another thing entirely. It involves meticulous planning and precision timing – just ask anyone who has put up a tent in a rainstorm. There are skills that must be learned, tasks that must be shared, and inevitable challenges to overcome. In other words, it's work. And where's the fun in that?

I've been camping for over twenty years, spending an average of one week a year under the billowing canvas. My enthusiasm for the "great outdoors" hasn't waned much over the years, but I do admit to making certain concessions to comfort, as I get older. For example, placing the sleeping bag directly on the ground was an adventure when I was very young. However, through the years I discovered that an inflatable

queen size bed is a much more comfortable solution.

Even at the ripe old age of "not yet dead," I remain a raving fan of camping and never tire of preaching  its virtues to the less adventurous. In a spiritual context, I believe it to be a well-worn path to Divinity or at least that part of the Divine which manifests in the natural world. One might argue that it is easier to find the gods of nature in the wild than it is to find them at the Hilton – even if the hotel does have a pool.

By following a few simple steps, anyone can experience the magic of camping:

#1: Choose wisely

Let's not get carried away by our new-found enthusiasm. Unless you are an experienced camper, I recommend that you stay away from primitive camping. Choose a public campground, one that has drive-up camping sites, restrooms, and shower facilities.

If you're in the US, visit www.reserveamerica.com where you'll find a comprehensive list of campgrounds, be able to check availability, choose your campsite, and even make reservations on-line. Doing some additional research on a specific campground can also prove beneficial. For example, a campground may look lovely on the internet, but, in reality, be situated next to a noisy highway. I prefer a wooded tent site, rather than open fields, as the trees above you will provide not only shade, but also shelter from rain. However, many campers prefer open spaces. If this is your first trip, I would recommend a two-night stay. One night is hardly worth the effort. Planning to stay for more than two nights is a gamble. You can always go back for more if you enjoy the experience.

#2: Plan carefully

You can never over-plan a camping trip. Start by making a list of items that you will need. The main list will likely evolve into multiple sub-lists, as you work through all the details in your mind. There may be a list of basic equipment, such as tent, sleeping bags, screen house, cooking utensils, portable grill, and so forth. Then a list of clothing and personal items needed for every member of the family. Then, finally, a grocery list (Planning meals that are easy to prepare in the woods is an entirely different topic!)

#3: Expect the unexpected

Follow the umbrella rule: If you pack an umbrella, it will not rain, but if you forget to pack the umbrella, it will pour. The same rule applies to first aid kits, warm clothing, and mosquitoes.

#4: Make friends with the park ranger

It is easy to dismiss the person in brown and green, who checks your name off the list as you drive into the campground. Don't. You may need him or her later. Furthermore, listen carefully to everything they tell you. Ignoring their advice may cause unnecessary problems for you and your party.

Rule #5: Have a plan B or, in other words, an exit strategy

In the unlikely event that the weather turns extreme or a member of your family becomes ill or a bear eats your tent, you should have a "break glass in emergency" plan. In times like these, the park ranger can quickly become your new best friend. At the very least, do some research in advance and know the location of the nearest hospital, not to mention the Hilton.

Rule #6: Make friends with the elements – all of them

Earth and Air and Fire and Water: camping will provide you and your family with a rare opportunity to experience the elements in an up close and personal way. Don't waste a second of this experience. This is what you came for and all of nature is ready and willing to enhance your experience.

Earth: although we tromp around on it all day, many of us fail to connect. When you place your tent on the ground and then later lay your head down to sleep, just inches from the forest floor, the sensation is much like laying your head down on your mother's bosom. You can almost hear the earth's heartbeat. Take time to kick off your shoes and feel the bare earth under your feet. Or as silly as it sounds, wrap your arms around a tree and place your face next to the bark. As you drift off to sleep at night listen to the sound of the wind in the tree above your head. Witches believe that the wind can speak to us; listen closely for your message, as it is whispered in the night.

Air: one of my favorite things to do when camping is simply to breathe. I take big, deep breaths of air, inhaling the unique smells of the wild places: pine trees, wood smoke, freshly mowed grass, and the heady perfume of wild flowers. The element of air is also manifest in the sky. Take time, while away from the clutter of everyday life, to really appreciate the world around you. Spread out in a green field and watch the clouds drift overhead or stare up at the starry sky after dark. Prepare to be amazed.

Fire: campfires are essential to a magical camping experience. There is nothing as exciting as sitting around a  campfire at night; the logs sparking and sputtering; the golden light of the fire illuminating the forest around you. You will feel as if you are suspended in a place between the worlds. Fire can also keep you warm. It can get cold in the woods at night.

Water: if you're fortunate enough to have a pond, river, or lake nearby, which is safe for recreational use – remember to check with your new best friend in the brown and green uniform – then by all means, enjoy. Many campers, however, become acquainted with this final element when it manifests as rain. Rain has the reputation of being similar to the unwanted guest at dinner. At the first sign of a rain drop, we are often ready to cash in our chips and head for home.

It is best to remember that rain is an essential part of the natural cycle: without it we would have no green forests or fertile fields. A good rule when camping is to count on rain to some degree. Make sure your tents are water resistant. If possible, arrange a covered communal space, such as a screen house, where the group can gather and stay reasonably dry. Take plenty of dry clothes and extra socks. But never get discouraged when it rains – it's all part of the camping experience.

#7: *Have fun*
Well, that's my hope anyway. If it all goes terribly wrong, then at least you can say you've tried it. Besides, sharing nature survival stories can be so entertaining at parties.

– JIMAHL DI FIOSA

Devils, Demons *and* Angels

THE WORDS *devil* and *demon* are not English words originally, but were borrowed from Greek. The English word *demon* was taken directly from the Latin *daemon*, which, in turn, goes back to the Greek *daímon* or *daimónion*. In Pagan Greece, a demon was a kind of immaterial or spiritual being who occupied a position in the universe midway between humanity and the Gods and could travel into either realm. Among other things, demons could serve as messengers between the two realms. These demons were not always malevolent, but quite often were benevolent or indifferent toward humanity.

The English word *devil* has a slightly more complicated history, going back to Old English (Anglo-Saxon) *deofol*, which is related to German *Teufel* and Dutch *duivel*. All three of these words can be traced back to the Gothic *diabaulus*. The Gothic word, in turn, was borrowed from Greek *diábolos*, which originally meant a slanderer, a liar, a perjurer, and so forth. That is, a *diábolos* is just a person – any ordinary person – who cast aspersions on others or spoke falsehoods.

The same Greek word was also borrowed into Latin as *diabolus*. As Latin evolved into French, Spanish, Portuguese and Italian, the Latin word became *diable* in French, *diablo* in Spanish, *diabo* in Portuguese and *diavolo* in Italian.

Angels are demons, too

Like so many other things, the meanings of these two words – *demon* and *devil* – were greatly changed by the coming of the monotheistic religions, Judaism and Christianity. The Hebrew Scriptures – including some books that the rabbis would later reject – began to be translated into Greek by Greek-speaking Jews, as early as the fourth century before the Christian era. This old Greek translation of the Hebrew Bible is usually called the Septuagint. It had an enormous influence on all the books of the New Testament, which were also written in Greek.

In the Septuagint, the kind of immaterial or spiritual Being that the Pagan Greeks called a demon is sometimes still called a demon (*daímon* or *daimónion*), More often, however, it is called an angel (*ángelos*). The Greek word *ángelos* just means a messenger, and it originally referred to ordinary people who carried messages. Applied to demons, the word just emphasizes one of the functions that those Beings have.

In the Septuagint, as in the New Testament, there was no moral difference whatsoever between a demon and an angel: an angel can be either good or evil, just as a demon can. The New Testament speaks in one place of "the devil and his angels" (Matthew 25:41). In another place, it describes a coming war in heaven, which the Archangel Michael and his angels will wage against Satan and his angels (Revelation 12:7, 9). The popular view that such Beings are called angels when they are good and messengers of the Christian or Jewish God, but demons when they are evil and messengers of the Devil, has no basis in the Bible. It is a somewhat later development, as we shall see below.

Satan, the adversary

In the Hebrew Scriptures, there is also the occasional mention of a being called *ha Satan*. This phrase just means "the adversary." In the Septuagint, however, Hebrew *ha Satan* is usually translated as *ho diábolos*, literally, "the slanderer, the liar." This is something of a mistranslation, but it seems to have been a traditional one. (In these phrases, the Hebrew *ha* or Greek *ho* simply means "the.")

The New Testament, being written in Greek and heavily influenced by the Septuagint, most often uses the same phrase, *ho diábolos*, "the Devil," to refer to the same Being. In a few places, however, he is called *ho Satanas*, which is simply a transcription (with a Greek ending added) of the Hebrew phrase *ha Satan*. Very rarely, he is simply called *Satanas*, without the word *ho* (meaning "the"). In these cases the word seems almost to be used as one of the Devil's proper names, Satan.

Demonizing the old gods

For monotheists, naturally enough, the many Gods and Goddesses of the Pagan Greeks could not be thought of as actual Gods, but had to be called by some other word. The early Christians, like the Jews, had no doubts about the existence of these Beings, but they saw them as subordinate Beings under their One God. Since the word *demon* originally referred to spiritual Beings subordinate to the Pagan Gods, Jewish monotheists, naturally enough, extended its range to cover the Pagan Gods as well. "For all the Gods of the Pagans are demons" – so claims the Septuagint (Psalm 95:5). (In the Hebrew and English Bibles, this is Psalm 96:5.)

Christians easily followed suit, beginning with Paul: Pagan sacrifices before images of their Gods are sacrifices "to demons (*daimónia*), not to God" (I Corinthians 10:20). Christians were to shun these sacrifices, which are a form of idolatry, as they would shun any sin. It is not too great a jump from all this to the notion that all the Pagan Gods are themselves evil Beings, and one small jump further turns every demon into an evil Being. And, of course, if all demons were evil, what should Christians call Beings of the same kind who serve their God? The word *angel* was at hand, and so it acquired its present, more limited meaning: angels good, demons bad.

– ROBERT MATHIESEN

TITANIA AND OBERON

O, woe, episode with an ass

THINGS GET drastic for the world when the king and queen of the fairies quarrel, especially on Midsummer Eve. At that astral time, magic prevails in the moonlight, attracting fairies and their ilk to throng in forests. The situation is, of course, primary to Shakespeare's *A Midsummer Night's Dream*, a journey through the hazards of love, the power of magic, and the marvel of dreams.

One legend tells us that Oberon was about three feet tall, carried a cockle shell as a shield, and wore a fish-scale coat of mail. Despite his diminutive size, the fairy king had enormous powers. He could read the future and like Zeus, his royal Olympian counterpart, could create terrifying lightning storms. Oberon sired Robin Goodfellow, who later fostered the race of mischievous sprites called Pucks.

Oberon's estranged queen, Titania, had formidable powers of her own and was in no way intimidated by her stormy spouse, although kings trump queens. The source of contention in the forest outside Athens that strange night was a charming Indian boy both wanted as a page. Titania vowed to keep the child because his mother, who had died in childbirth, had been her follower. Their battle had raged on and on, evoking a world of chaos:

The ox hath therefore stretched his yoke in vain,
The plowman lost his sweat, and the green corn
Hath rotted ere his youth attained a beard:
The fold stands empty in the drowned field,
And crows are fatted with the murrion flock.

The "murrion flock" are herds of sheep and cattle infected with plague. So had psychic rage infected the earth.

On that infamous night, Oberon recruits Puck to help wreak revenge on the disobedient Titania. When she is asleep in her bower, Puck sprinkles on her eyelids a juice made from flowers called "love-in-idleness." Awakened, she will fall in love with the first creature she sees.

Meanwhile the interlocking plots thicken, and love as well as rage befog the air. The fairies have gathered to attend the nuptials on the following morning of Theseus, the king of

Athens, and Hippolyta, queen of the Amazons. Two sets of lovers stumble through the woods in a state of bewilderment and emotional errors – Puck has caused comic misadventures with magic misapplied. While this amorous confusion compounds, a band of "rude mechanicals" also blunders around the forest. Nick Bottom, the weaver, and the other bumpkin artisans are rehearsing a bumbling pageant; traditionally laborers were hired to "entertain" wedding guests.

Now Puck's mischief reaches new heights of the ridiculous. The head of an ass appears on Bottom, and the fairy queen awakens to his braying attempt at song. It is love at first sight.

*Come, sit thee down upon this
     flowery bed,*

While I thy amiable cheeks do coy,

*And stick musk-roses on thy
     sleek, smooth head,*

*And kiss thy fair large ears, my
     gentle joy.*

Titania sets her retinue – Peaseblossom, Moth, Cobweb and Mustardseed – to fetch Bottom the feast he chooses, oats and a bottle of hay. The ass is overwhelmed by bliss when Titania, beautiful beyond his wildest imagination, caresses him and tells him, "O, how I love thee! I dote on thee!"

The rest of the night passes in such improbability. With the sun, harmony also arises.

The lovers are properly sorted out in couples and will join Theseus and Hippolyta in a triple wedding. At the sight of Titania petting the ass, Oberon feels remorse and releases her from the spell. Titania is appalled at her beastly indiscretion, and she and Oberon reconcile. Titania gives him the boy, Oberon will share his kingdom with her, and the world will be relieved of its dismal spell. The weaver is relieved of his physically asinine appearance and dimly remembers an outlandish fantasy. He and the other rustics enact a "most lamentable comedy," hilariously inept and good naturedly received by the wedding guests. Titania and Oberon bless the royal house, its newlyweds, and the future offspring of the couples. The creatures of the Midsummer Night's confusions believe they have been dreaming, and as we learn elsewhere, all's well that ends well.

– BARBARA STACY

From our publication Greek Gods in Love *by Barbara Stacy. To read other stories from the book, visit our website www.TheWitchesAlmanac.com/ greekgodsinlove.html*

Easy Time Changes

Presage and the Moon Calendar for the world community

A FAMOUS scene from the classic film *The Wizard of Oz* comes to mind in considering the complex and intriguing topic of time and astrology. Dorothy and Toto, standing on the Yellow Brick Road in Munchkin Land, are advised that it's always best to begin at the beginning. *Witches' Almanac* readers from around the world – Australia, the UK, Brazil – and around the USA have frequently asked whether they can use the astrological information in Presage and the Moon Calendar. The answer is an enthusiastic "yes!" And it really is easy to do so just by starting at the beginning. The astrological information for the *Almanac* is always calculated for Eastern Standard and Daylight Time. This is the time zone which is in effect in Providence, Rhode Island where the *Almanac* is headquartered.

So, let's say "to Oz!" and look at the road to follow in order to determine what time this is in other places. The tables used by astrologers to determine the day-to-day positions of the Sun, Moon and planets are all calculated for Universal or Greenwich Mean Time, the world standard time meridian. It begins in Greenwich, England. Including daylight saving and war time variations in different years and half hour time zones corrections, there are about 45 different time zones in use around the planet. The International Date Line, which runs North and South and is generally marked on globes and maps by a thin line, can be located by looking between Alaska and Russia. This determines when one day becomes the next.

The planets move a degree or less during the span of a day, and there are thirty degrees in each zodiac sign. The birth sign forecasts in Presage are prepared so that *Almanac* readers everywhere can relate to the overall message in the given time frame. The Moon Calendar requires a little bit of adjustment though. So will the section listing the eclipses, which are always exactly at a New or Full Moon. The Moon moves rapidly, about one degree every two hours. It remains in each sign for a little over two days, completing the circuit of all twelve zodiac signs about every twenty-eight days.

Readers in the UK and Australia will be ahead of this time correction while those in most of the other time zones in the Americas (except for Atlantic Standard Time) will be behind. Use the chart below for a quick glance at how to correct the Moon Calendar in some familiar time zones. Occasionally, readers will have to correct the Moon's sign by one day. Readers in Australia and China should look back to the Moon sign on the previous day. In Hawaii, look ahead at the next day.

To make certain your calculations are correct, a wonderful free website is available, The World Time Clock & Map at http://24timezones.com. At a glance this allows you to compare your own time zone to the East Coast, USA time. The Daylight Saving Time corrections around the world are listed too. A sidebar on The World Time Clock shows the constantly changing time corrections currently in effect. It offers a fascinating glimpse into just how fluid and illusionary the concept of clock time really is.

–DIKKI-JO MULLEN

12:00 PM Universal Time (England)

7:00 AM Eastern Standard Time (New York)
Remember, this is the time zone used in the Moon Calendar and Presage.
Daylight Saving Time corrections are included.

6:00 AM Central Standard Time (Chicago)

5:00 AM Mountain Standard Time (Denver)

4:00 AM Pacific Standard Time (Los Angeles)

1:00 AM Alaskan Hawaiian Standard Time (Honolulu)

1:00 PM Central European Time (Paris)

5:30 PM Indian Time (Mumbai, India)

8:00 PM Australian Western Time (Perth, Australia and also Beijing, China)

10:00 PM Australian Eastern Time (Melbourne, Australia)

MOON GARDENING

BY PHASE

Sow, transplant, bud and graft		*Plow, cultivate, weed and reap*		
NEW	First Quarter	FULL	Last Quarter	NEW
Plant above-ground crops with outside seeds, flowering annuals.	Plant above-ground crops with inside seeds.	Plant root crops, bulbs, biennials, perennials.		Do not plant.

BY PLACE IN THE ZODIAC

Fruitful Signs

Cancer – Most favorable planting time for all leafy crops bearing fruit above ground. Prune to encourage growth in Cancer.

Scorpio – Second only to Cancer, a Scorpion Moon promises good germination and swift growth. In Scorpio, prune for bud development.

Pisces – Planting in the last of the Watery Triad is especially effective for root growth.

Taurus – The best time to plant root crops is when the Moon is in the sign of the Bull.

Capricorn – The Earthy Goat Moon promotes the growth of rhizomes, bulbs, roots, tubers and stalks. Prune now to strengthen branches.

Libra – Airy Libra may be the least beneficial of the Fruitful Signs, but is excellent for planting flowers and vines.

Barren Signs

Leo – Foremost of the Barren Signs, the Lion Moon is the best time to effectively destroy weeds and pests. Cultivate and till the soil.

Gemini – Harvest in the Airy Twins; gather herbs and roots. Reap when the Moon is in a sign of Air or Fire to assure best storage.

Virgo – Plow, cultivate, and control weeds and pests when the moon is in Virgo.

Sagittarius – Plow and cultivate the soil or harvest under the Archer Moon. Prune now to discourage growth.

Aquarius – This dry sign of Air is perfect for ground cultivation, reaping crops, gathering roots and herbs. It is a good time to destroy weeds and pests.

Aries – Cultivate, weed, and prune to lessen growth. Gather herbs and roots for storage.

Consult our Moon Calendar pages for phase and place in the zodiac circle. The Moon remains in a sign for about two-and-a-half days. Match your gardening activity to the day that follows the Moon's entry into that zodiac sign.

The MOON Calendar

is divided into zodiac signs rather than the more familiar Gregorian calendar.

♈ 2014

♓ 2015

Bear in mind that new projects should be initiated when the Moon is waxing (from dark to full). When the Moon is on the wane (from full to dark), it is a time for storing energy and the wise person waits.

Please note that Moons are listed by day of entry into each sign. Quarters are marked, but as rising and setting times vary from one region to another, it is advisable to check your local newspaper, library or planetarium.
The Moon's Place is computed for Eastern Standard Time.

Key to the Kingdom

This is the key to the kingdom. In that kingdom there is a city. In that city there is a town. In that town there is a street. In that street there is a lane. In that lane there is a yard. In that yard there is a house. In that house there is a room. In that room there is a bed. On that bed there is a basket. In that basket there are some flowers. Flowers in the basket, basket on the bed, bed in the room, etc. etc.

THIS ANTIQUE nursery rhyme, forward and backward, states a simple truth. A room of your own is a key to the kingdom of happiness. Your room can be a place of comfort and delight. Fill it with your favorite colors, books, pictures, music, scent – let its atmosphere become an extension of yourself. Your room can cheer you in morning light, comfort you at day's end and become a haven when the outside world of natural and human forces turns hostile. Many ancient rituals and quaint old customs devised to bless and protect your room can be found in the occult archives.

If you sense something amiss, or if unpleasant vibrations invade your room, you might try a remedy many witches swear by. Take a peeled clove of garlic and slice it lengthwise with a sharp knife. Leave it on a saucer in the room for a day and a night until it has absorbed the evil influences. A similar recipe recommends using an onion, quartered. After the garlic or onion have done their work, burn them but avoid inhaling the fumes.

To create harmony and make the room truly your own, a formal ceremony can be performed. The following blessing rite should take place when the sun is in your natal sign and the moon occupies one of the Earth signs – Taurus, Virgo, Capricorn – and is waxing to full. Locate the cardinal points with a compass and mark the east, south, west and north quarters so they may be easily seen from the center of the room where you will position yourself to carry out the simple ritual. You will need a white candle and a small bowl of salted water. At midnight, darken the room and light the candle. Dip your fingers in the salted water and with four fingers and thumb pressed tightly together, touch your forehead, lips and heart. From the center of the room, hold out the lighted candle to each of the four quarters in turn as you say:

Winds of the east, blow gently,
Winds of the south, blow fair,
Winds of the west, cease and rest,
Winds of the north, take care.

Facing east and holding the candle high above your head, complete the ceremony with these words: *Whirling, changing winds of fate, guard my dwelling place now and evermore.*

– Originally published in the 1979/1980 Witches' Almanac.

capricorn

December 21 – January 19
Cardinal Sign of Earth ∀ Ruled by Saturn ♄

S	M	T	W	T	F	S
☽ **WAXING** As the Moon increases, its form takes the shape of the capital letter D: D for Daring… a time for creativity, expansion, and development… Later on as darkness falls, it shines like a beacon of hope, raising your spirits and assuring the success of your ventures. –Celtic Tree Magic						DEC. 21 Winter Solstice ❄
22 Gather holly	23 Virgo	24 The wheel turns	25 ◑ Libra	26	27 Johannes Kepler born, 1571 Scorpio	28
29 Sagittarius	30	31 Touch a pine tree Capricorn	JAN. 1 ● 2014	2 WAXING Aquarius	3 Wish upon the moon	4 Jacob Grimm born, 1785 Pisces
5	6 Don't tempt fate Aries	7 ◐	8 Gather snow	9 Feast of Janus Taurus	10 Gift a talisman	11 Gemini
12 A chill	13	14 Fly by night Cancer	15 ◯ Wolf Moon	16 WANING Leo	17	18 Make a sacrifice
19 Virgo	**WANING** Rising later night after night, the Moon diminishes in size, now assuming the form of the letter C: C for Caring. The time has come to relax, restore energy, and quietly dispel negative influences in your life. Banish fear as the Moon wanes. – excerpt from Moon Lore ☽					

45

The Cornish Yarrow Spell

ON THE NEW MOON or even on the evening before, a young girl shall place a piece of yarrow herb under her pillow with the intention of knowing her true love. Recite the spell:

Good night, fair yarrow,
Thrice good night to thee;
I hope before tomorrow's dawn
My true love I shall see.

If a marriage to one she already knows is in the stars, the girl shall see her intended true love on the following morning.

aquarius

January 20 – February 18

Fixed Sign of Air △ Ruled by Uranus ♅

S	M	T	W	T	F	S
	JAN. 20	21 May evil recede Libra	22	23	24 Scorpio	25 Love passionately
26 Burn old habits Sagittarius	27	28 Alan Alda born, 1936 Capricorn	29 Wish on the new moon	30 Aquarius	31 WAXING Year of the Horse	FEB. 1 Oimelc Eve Pisces
2 Candlemas	3 Treat your familiar Aries	4	5 Open a new door Taurus	6	7 Embrace change Gemini	8
9	10 Prepare moon candles Cancer	11	12 Abraham Lincoln born, 1809 Leo	13	14 Storm Moon	15 Lupercalia WANING Virgo
16 Embrace love	17 Sign no documents Libra	18 Ring bells				

MOON PASSAGE

Once long ago humans depended upon the Moon for reckoning time, planting crops and harvesting the sea... In a sense the lovely silver sphere... is more mysterious now despite the exploration of its surface. The Moon's curious forces continue to exert their influence over us and our planet. We and the oceans of Earth still unceasingly respond to the Moon's magnetic appeal. As a symbol of mystic significance, appreciated by so many ancient religious expressions, the Moon remains as potent as ever, at least to the poet, the artist and the witch. - excerpt from *Moon Lore*

Enchanted Porridge

LONG AGO, on the edge of the forest, there lived a sickly woman and her devoted daughter. The daughter was a virtuous and compassionate soul, who cared tirelessly for her mother. But as the harsh winter progressed, the duo's situation became increasingly desperate. Soon they were down to their last pot of porridge.

Facing starvation, the young woman reluctantly left her mother's side, slipping into the forest to search for nature's last scraps. She dug in the crisp snow, looking for roots. She shook the frost off branches hoping to uncover a few frozen berries. She tried to find anything that might sustain them, but the landscape was as depleted as her cupboards.

Just as the young woman was beginning to lose all hope, the scent of sweet porridge suddenly filled her nostrils. She ran towards its source to discover an old woman eating porridge from a large iron pot.

"Please ma'am, may I have some of your porridge? I'm rather famished and fear I won't have the strength to walk back to my sick mother – she's waiting for me in our cottage. Please?"

"Well," replied the old woman, "since you asked so nicely, take the whole pot! Take it home to your ailing mother. She is sure to improve with a steady diet of hearty porridge. Just say 'please' whenever you are hungry and the pot will cook as much porridge as you want. When you've had your fill, say the other magic words and the pot will stop cooking."

Overjoyed, the girl thanked the old woman profusely. She quickly set about dragging the cumbersome pot back home. The old woman proved correct about the salubrious qualities of porridge: the sickly mother was fast improving. The young woman cooked porridge in the enchanted pot three times a day, asking only for as much as they needed.

One day, as the young woman was gathering firewood, her mother decided she was well enough to fix her own porridge. She had seen her daughter start cooking several times, so she walked confidently to the pot and said "please." She ate until she was content, but the porridge kept coming.

"Okay," said the mother, "that's enough! No more porridge! Stop!"

But it kept coming, until the entire house was filled with porridge! By the time the daughter returned, porridge was flowing from the windows. "I'm sorry, dear! I didn't know what to say to make it stop!"

"That's okay, Mother," said the girl kindly. "Just say 'Thank you!'"

And with that the porridge ceased to flow. The duo spent the better part of the next three days eating their way back into their cottage, but they did not mind in the least: they were grateful for everything they had!

– THE GRIMM BROTHERS,
retelling by SHANNON MARKS

pisces
February 19 – March 20
Mutable Sign of Water ▽ Ruled by Neptune ♆

S	M	T	W	T	F	S
SELENE ...*Selene persuades Zeus to grant her beloved one wish. Endymion chooses perpetual youth by means (continued below)*			Feb. 19	20 Scorpio	21	22 Sagittarius
23 *Wear the color of the sun*	24 *Winslow Homer born, 1836* Capricorn	25	26 Aquarius	27 *Assemble at the crossroads*	28 *Matronalia* ⇨ Pisces	March 1
2 WAXING Aries	3 *Search early memories*	4 Taurus	5 *Decorate a tree*	6	7 Gemini	8
9 *Daylight Savings Time begins @ 2am* Cancer	10 *Bathe in blue water*	11	12 *Vaslav Nijinsky born, 1890* Leo	13	14 Virgo	15 *Assemble at the 13th hour*
16 Chaste Moon	17 WANING Libra	18 *Unlucky day*	19 *Minerva's Day* Scorpio	20		

of perpetual sleep, and retires to a deep underground cave. In another, it is Selene who imposes everlasting sleep on her handsome lover. Whichever, Endymion must have been aroused on occasion, as all sources agree that he fathered fifty daughters with the goddess. And when the Moon wanes, it is said that Selene visits her lover deep in his cavern of repose.   – excerpt from *Moon Lore*

49

Old Country Rhyme

Beachwood fires are bright and clear,
If the logs are kept a year;
Chestnut only good they say,
If for long it's laid away;
Make a fire of elder tree,
Death within your house shall be;
But ash new or ash old
Is fit for Queen with crown of gold.

Birch and fir logs burn too fast,
Blaze up bright and do not last;
It is by the Irish said
Hawthorn bakes the sweetest bread.
Elmwood burns like churchyard mould –
E'en the very flames are cold;
But ash green or ash brown
Is fit for Queen with golden crown.

Poplar gives a bitter smoke,
Fills your eyes and makes you choke;
Apple wood will scent your room
With an incense-like perfume;
Oaken logs, if dry and old,
Keep away the winter's cold;
But ash wet or ash dry
A King shall warm his slippers by.

aries

March 20 – April 19

Cardinal Sign of Fire △ Ruled by Mars ♂

S	M	T	W	T	F	S
FEARN (ALDER) *The alder is usually found thriving in thickets beside lakes, streams and rivers. It so favors marshy conditions that the tree seldom grows on drier land. (continued below)*				MAR. 20 2014 Vernal Equinox Scorpio	21 *Warm by a fire*	22 Sagittarius
23 ◑	24 Capricorn	25 *Bela Bartok born, 1881*	26 Aquarius	27 *Smile often*	28 Pisces	29 *Plan your garden*
30 ● Aries	31 WAXING	APRIL 1 All Fools' Day Taurus	2	3 Gemini	4 *Sing a song*	5
6 *Merle Haggard born, 1937* Cancer	7 ◐	8 *Patience, patience* Leo	9	10 *Enjoy hot tea*	11 *Planting day!* Virgo	12 *Read about flowers*
13 *Bless the soil* Libra	14 Total lunar eclipse ⇨	15 ◯ Seed Moon	16 WANING Scorpio	17	18 *Cast the runes* Sagittarius	19

*The alder is associated with Bran, a Celtic hero/god. One tale about him is found in the medieval Welsh collection of legends known as **The Mabinogion**. Another story, **The Voyage of Bran to the World Below**, occurs in Irish literature recorded in the 8th century.* – excerpt from *Celtic Tree Magic*

51

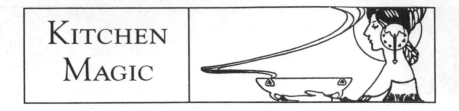
Chia Seeds

IT SEEMS THAT we modern folk are constantly rediscovering what the ancients already knew. Witness, for example, the recent surge in popularity of chia seeds. Yes, those ch-ch-chia seeds. Once relegated to the realm of novelty, chia seeds are now being touted as "the ultimate super-food" and "the new flax."

However, there is nothing new about chia. Cultivated extensively in ancient Mesoamerica, chia, or *Salvia hispanica*, was consumed by Aztec warriors. Packed with Omega3 fatty acids, protein, fiber, calcium and other nutrients, chia has been linked to such health benefits as increased stamina, reduced anxiety, weight loss through appetite suppression, and improved cardiovascular health.

So why was such a potent food lost in time? The clash of cultures that occurred when the Spanish began their colonization of the Americas resulted in the active suppression of certain native practices. Chia may have been a casualty because of its use in religious rites. Viewed as a threat to the Church, cultivation and use were suppressed.

Among the reasons chia has once again gained popularity is because it is so easy to incorporate into your diet.

The tiny, almost tasteless seeds can be stirred into oatmeal, sprinkled in salad or ground up and added to flour for baking cookies or breads. They can also simply be dropped into a cup of water to form "chia gel" that can then be consumed straight or added to almost anything you cook.

As with all health food trends, however, one should be careful: chia may interfere with certain medications, such as those that regulate blood pressure and glucose levels. Consult your doctor or nutritionist before making significant changes to your diet.

Chia gel:
Simply stir one tablespoon of chia seeds into one cup of water, let rest and stir again. Chia gel should be stored in a refrigerated airtight container.

Chia fresca:
A variant of the *Aguas Fresca* served in Mexico and Central America. Mix 12 oz water, the juice of one lime, a bit of lime zest, one teaspoon whole chia seeds, and the sweetener of your choice – we recommend a touch of agave nectar. Shake well and pour over ice. Enjoy on a hot day for a refreshing boost!

– SHANNON MARKS

taurus

April 20 – May 20
Fixed Sign of Earth ♅ Ruled by Venus ♀

S	M	T	W	T	F	S
April 20 Tend the hedge Capricorn	21	22 ◐ Aquarius	23 Toss a coin	24 Pisces	25 Cast a spell	26 Carol Burnett born, 1935 Aries
27 Honor the moon	28 Partial solar eclipse ⇨	29 ● Taurus	30 WAXING Walpurgis Night	May 1 Beltane Gemini	2 Eat honey	3 Cancer
4	5 Søren Kierkegaard born, 1813	6 ◖ Leo	7 Wear red	8 Virgo	9	10 Beware of enemies
11 Judge no one Libra	12	13 Vesak Day ⇨ Scorpio	14 ◯ Hare Moon	15 WANING Sagittarius	16 Gossip hurts	17 Clouds gather Capricorn
18	19 Pray for rain Aquarius	20				

SAILLE (WILLOW)

An Old Testament reference to the exiled Jews hanging their harps upon the willows as they wept beside the rivers of Babylon led to the weeping willow's classification by Linnaeus as Silax babylonica. In ancient Greece, the goddess Hera was born under a willow on the island of Samos, where a magnificent temple was built to honor her. The willow of the Druids was not the weeping willow, but the tree or shrub we know as the pussy willow.

– excerpt from Celtic Tree Magic

53

Boys and Girls Bookshelf *(New York, NY: The University Society, 1920)*

gemini

May 21 – June 20

Mutable Sign of Air △ Ruled by Mercury ☿

S	M	T	W	T	F	S
			MAY 21 ◑ Pisces	22 Sir Lawrence Olivier born, 1907	23 Take flight	24 Aries
25 WANING	26 Taurus	27 Draw on cloud power	28 ● Gemini	29 WAXING Oak Apple Day	30 Cancer	31 Record dreams
JUNE 1 Turn a coin	2 Leo	3 Know your past	4 Night of the Watchers ⇨	5 ◐ Virgo	6 Alexander Pushkin born, 1799	7 Libra
8 Revenge?	9 Scorpio	10	11 Accept your destiny	12 Sagittarius	13 Dyad Moon	14 WANING Capricorn
15 Beware of crows	16 Aquarius	17 Make incense	18 Pisces	19 ◐	20 Gather St. Johnswort Aries

uath (hawthorn)

Hawthorn is so strongly associated with the Celtic May Eve festival that "may" is a folk name for it. Whitethorn is another name popular in Brittany, where the tree marks fairy trysting places. Sacred hawthorns guard wishing wells in Ireland, where shreds of clothing are hung on the thorns to symbolize a wish made. – excerpt from Celtic Tree Magic

Babyhood Superstitions of New England

An open hand in a baby is a sign of a generous disposition, but a habit of closing the fingers indicates avarice, or, as we say, close-fistedness.
— Cambridge, Massachusetts

The baby must go upstairs before it goes downstairs, or it will never rise in the world. *— Massachusetts*

A baby should not look into a glass before it is a year old; if it does it will die. *— Deer Isle, Maine*

First a son, then a daughter, you've begun just as you oughter.
— Brookline, Massachusetts

One article of an unborn infant's wardrobe must be left unmade or unbought or the child is liable not to live.
— Salem, Massachusetts

Rock the cradle empty, have children a plenty. Rock the chair empty, have sickness a plenty.
— Nashua, New Hampshire

The first time a baby is taken visiting, if it is laid on a married couple's bed there will be a baby for that couple.
— Salem, Massachusetts

A child's tumbling out of bed is a sign he will never be a fool.
— Maine

If a child "favors its father," it is good luck for it. It will get on well in the world. *— Salem, Massachusetts*

— EDITED BY FANNY D. BERGEN

cancer
June 21 – July 22
Cardinal Sign of Water ▽ Ruled by Moon ☽

CANCER

S	M	T	W	T	F	S

ÐUIR (OAK)

Long held sacred, the oak was dedicated by the Greeks to Zeus, the Romans to Jupiter, and the Norsemen to Thor – all gods of the lightning flash. The acorn in mystic lore represents the highest form of fertility – creativity of the mind. — excerpt from *Celtic Tree Magic*

JUNE 21 Summer Solstice ☼

S	M	T	W	T	F	S
22 Gower Champion born, 1921 Taurus	23	24 Midsummer	25 Talk to a pixie Gemini	26	27 ● Cancer	28 WAXING
29 Light a candle Leo	30	JULY 1 Gather berries	2 Offer advice Virgo	3	4 Assess goals Libra	5 ◑
6	7 Don't mask fear Scorpio	8	9 Avoid jasper Sagittarius	10	11 Capricorn	12 ○ Mead Moon
13 WANING Aquarius	14	15 Pisces	16 Plan a party	17 Erle Stanley Gardner born, 1889 Aries	18 ◐	19 Taurus
20	21 Treat yourself Gemini	22 Star gaze				

TAROT'S EMPEROR

THE EMPEROR.

THE EMPEROR is the pinnacle of masculinity, a sovereign in every sense: an outstanding leader, rich in wealth and character, boldly breaking new ground, whether through overt aggression or clever diplomacy. His power is absolute and unquestioned, earned through a lifetime of careful decision making and self-regulation. The Emperor desires order, structure, and procedure: an empire must be disciplined in order to function properly. The Emperor is the arbiter of this discipline.

Card number four of the Major Arcana, the Emperor is stable and practical, preferring reasoned thinking over emotional reaction. In general, the Emperor indicates a need for discipline. Is your workplace frenetic? Are your finances organized? Focus on the chaotic aspects of your life and work towards balanced solutions.

leo

July 23 – August 22

Fixed Sign of Fire △ Ruled by Sun ☉

S	M	T	W	T	F	S
			JULY 23 Ancient Egyptian New Year	24 Cancer	25 Bury a curse	26 ● Leo
27 WAXING Watch sunrise	28 Joe E. Brown born, 1892	29 Virgo	30 Honor the Sun	31 Lughnassad Eve Libra	AUGUST 1 Lammas	2
3 ◐ Scorpio	4	5 Tempers flare Sagittarius	6	7 Carry three pebbles Capricorn	8	9 Visit a river Aquarius
10 ○ Wort Moon	11 WANING Pisces	12 Dreams are remembered	13 Diana's Day Aries	14	15 Thomas de Quincey born, 1785 Taurus	16
17 ◑	18 Black Cat Appreciation ⇐Day Gemini	19 Avoid over-sensitivity	20 Cancer	21	22	

TINNE (HOLLY)

The holly had a strong association with divination in Northern Europe. A charm to bring a dream of your future mate required nine spiky leaves of holly collected at midnight before moonrise. Complete silence was to be observed as you wrapped the leaves in a square of pure white linen, placed the packet under your pillow and dreamed the night away. — excerpt from *Celtic Tree Magic*

The Farmer and the Gnome

FARMER John was very excited: after years of working his papa's farm, he was finally striking out on his own to a derelict farm house on the edge of the woods. The fields hadn't been plowed for ages and in fact resembled a miniature mountain range. Still, Farmer John was optimistic, especially since the farmhouse itself – although unoccupied for at least a decade – was still in perfect condition. Even the window sills looked as though they had been freshly cleaned.

So Farmer John set about plowing the fields. He plowed day and night until the fields were as smooth and straight as a placid lake – except for one stubborn mound of dirt. No matter how many times he brought his plow over the mound, it would not budge. So Farmer John grabbed his pick ax and started swinging. After a few hearty blows, the mound began to crack open and Farmer John discovered that it was hollow inside.

Inside he discovered a small den, completely furnished and rather cozy. On the walls hung tiny tools from tiny hooks; a tiny smokeless fire crackled in an open pit; in front of the fire sat a threadbare recliner; and on the stool next to the armchair rested the smallest pipe Farmer John had ever seen. It was no bigger than Farmer John's thumbnail and still wafting sweet wisps of cherry scented tobacco.

Farmer John knew at once that he had just destroyed a gnome's home, the very gnome who had probably been maintaining the farmhouse all these years. Farmer John knew, too, that, it being daylight, the gnome was tucked away somewhere inside, hiding from the mad man who had just torn open his burrow! And Farmer John especially knew that he was in big trouble.

So Farmer John yelled a heartfelt "sorry!" into the gnome's den and then ran into the farmhouse. He quickly buttered some bread and ran back to the mound, placing the offering inside the now busted home. "There's more in the farmhouse, Mister Gnome! Please come inside tonight and I'll give you some more! There's a special entrance for you on the west side. Please don't be mad!"

Farmer John never waited for nightfall with as much trepidation as he did that night. He was sure the gnome would punish him somehow. But the night came and went without incidence and the next morning, when Farmer John awoke to make breakfast, he discovered all the butter missing from the icebox, and in its place a note: *Dear Farmer John: Thanks for your butter and your concern. Nothing a little hard work couldn't fix. Yours truly, the Gnome.*

– SHANNON MARKS

virgo
August 23 – September 21
Mutable Sign of Earth ▽ Ruled by Mercury ☿

S	M	T	W	T	F	S
COLL (hazel) *The staff of the Roman god Mercury was of hazel wood. The myths say Apollo presented the caduceus to Hermes, the Greek (continued below)*						**Aug. 23** Leo
24	25 ● Virgo	26 WAXING	27 *Georg Hegel born, 1770*	28 Libra	29 Ganesh Festival	30 Scorpio
31	**Sept. 1** *Be patient*	2 ◑ Sagittarius	3	4 *Ward off evil* Capricorn	5	6 *Thoughts take flight* Aquarius
7	8 (Barley Moon) Pisces	9 WANING	10 Aries	11	12 *Maurice Chevalier born, 1888* Taurus	13 *Harvest herbs*
14 Gemini	15 ◐	16 Cancer	17 *Bake twin pies*	18	19 *Kiss your love* Leo	20
21 *Make magic!*	22 Virgo	counterpart of Mercury, in recognition of his mystical power to calm human passion and improve virtue. The medieval magician's wand was traditionally cut from the hazel tree with scrupulous ceremony drawn from Hebraic sources. Ancient Irish heralds carried white hazel wands. — excerpt from *Celtic Tree Magic*				

Love & the Apple

Apple seeds

WHEN EATING an apple, snap it with the fingers and name it for a person. Count the fully developed seeds (all of the others are kisses), and the last one must correspond to the following formula:

One's my love,
Two's my love,
Three's my heart's desire.
Four I'll take and never forsake,
Five I'll cast in the fire.
Six he loves,
Seven she loves,
Eight they both love,
Nine he comes,
Ten he tarries,
Eleven he goes,
Twelve he marries.
Thirteen honor,
Fourteen riches,
All the rest are little witches.

Some change the latter lines of this formula into:

Thirteen they quarrel,
Fourteen they part,
Fifteen they die with a broken heart.

libra

September 22 – October 22

Cardinal Sign of Air ♎ Ruled by Venus ♀

LIBRA

S	M	T	W	T	F	S
		Sept. 23 Autumnal Equinox ♌	24 ● Libra	25 WAXING	26 Passionate hearts collide Scorpio	27
28 Take a chance	29 Sagittarius	30	Oct. 1 ◑ Capricorn	2 Jack Parsons born, 1914	3 Aquarius	4 Time for study
5 Pisces	6 Gaze at the moon	7 Total lunar eclipse ⇨ Aries	8 Blood Moon	9 WAXING Taurus	10 Act quickly	11 Gemini
12	13	14 Enjoy folly Cancer	15 ◐	16 Noah Webster born, 1758 Leo	17	18
19 Try to behave Virgo	20	21	22 Cast a spell Libra			

MUIN (VINE)

Celtic scholars now agree that the "vine" of the Druidic tree alphabet refers to the blackberry bramble bush. The sacred nature of the blackberry is evidenced in old tales and heathen customs observed down through the centuries. A loop of blackberry bramble served as a healing source in much the same way as a holed stone. Traditional rites involved passing a baby through the loop three times to secure good health. One ancient legend tells how blackberries gathered and eaten within the span of the waxing moon at harvest time assured protection from the force of evil runes. – excerpt from Celtic Tree Magic

Patchouli

PATCHOULI first came to Western attention during the eighteenth century, when the herb traveled from the east along the Silk Road, wrapped in the eponymous fabric. Patchouli not only repelled the insects who were keen to nibble the valuable silk, but lent an exotic aroma to the wares. A most agreeable aphrodisiac, patchouli quite literally seduced the buyers. Its distinctive, earthy odor became high fashion in European courts, considered evocative of imported luxury and untroubled existence.

Patchouli remains popular. It is a common ingredient in perfumes and incense, as its alluring scent is simultaneously calming and stimulating. Patchouli is a useful herb for meditation, as its aroma serves to ground the practitioner.

Patchouli is said to increase desire while reducing anxiety, creating a heady cocktail of free thoughts and lowered inhibitions. The herb's aphrodisiac properties made it popular among practitioners of free love. The scent of patchouli can reputedly relieve stress, anxiety, sexual dysfunction, and depression. Because of patchouli's antibacterial and anti-inflammatory properties, the herb and its essential oil are multifaceted medicines.

Patchouli is particularly beneficial in ointments for soothing dry or irritated skin. It can also speed up the healing process of cuts and abrasions. Patchouli is also valuable from a purely cosmetic standpoint: regular applications can make the skin soft, smooth, and supple.

A native of tropical Asia, patchouli is ruled by Saturn. Patchouli is used in rituals to help break bad habits; to meditate on the direction of one's life; and to seek protection from forces that threaten mental and physical health.

Because Patchouli and its ruler Saturn are so strongly associated with forces of grounding, this potent herb is used to manifest something in the physical realm, especially money. For example, use patchouli oil to draw a money symbol on a blank index card. Fold the card in half three times and then place it in your wallet or wherever you carry money. As you carry the card, visualize it growing bigger and bigger and finally bursting. Money will soon find its way to your pockets. But always use caution when imploring Saturn for monetary gain: he will only allow you to reap what you have sown. In other words, your reward must be earned through centered attention and self-awareness.

Patchouli, love it or hate it, has stood the test of time. Its musky aroma will surely be with us for centuries to come.

– TENEBROUS RAE

scorpio
October 23 – November 21
Fixed Sign of Water ▽ Ruled by Pluto ♀

ſCORPIVſ

S	M	T	W	T	F	S
GORT (IVY) *The rich deep evergreen color and climbing spiral action... identify ivy with immortality, resurrection and rebirth.* – excerpt from Celtic Tree Magic				Oct. 23 Scorpio	24 Partial solar ⇐ eclipse	25 WAXING
26 Sagittarius	27	28 Jonas Salk born, 1914 Capricorn	29 Sing to the dead	30 Aquarius	31 Samhain Eve	Nov. 1 Hallowmas
2 Daylight Savings Time ends @ 2am Pisces	3 Visit a cemetery	4 Aries	5 Give a gift to the moon	6 Snow Moon Taurus	7 WANING	8 Locate Sirius Gemini
9	10 Cook for a friend Cancer	11	12 Hold your tongue	13 Leo	14	15 Virgo
16 Hecate Night	17	18 Libra	19 J.R. Capablanca born, 1888	20 Scorpio	21 Celebrate love	

NGETAL (REED)

Pan pursued the nymph [Syrinx] from mountain to river, where she eluded him by becoming a reed. The god, bewildered by the myriad reeds and unable to recognize her among them, cut several of the plants at random – and out of these, to turn his lust and sorrow into song, devised the glorious panpipe. – excerpt from Celtic Tree Magic

YEAR OF THE WOOD HORSE
January 31, 2014 – February 18, 2015

THE OLDEST of the world's zodiacs follows a cycle of twelve years. The legend is that Buddha invited all of the animals to his birthday party. The twelve who came were each rewarded with a year and the promise that they would be the animals to hide in the hearts of those born that year. The Horse is the seventh of the twelve animals Buddha rewarded with steward-ship. Five elements (fire, water, metal, earth, and wood) distinguish the animals. Every sixty years the pattern of element and animal pairs repeats. Strong-willed and earthy, the Wood Horse tosses its head with determina-tion. This is the year to act upon new ideas and inspirations. Innovative techniques, courage, and using the element of surprise will lead to winning situations. Remember the legend of the Trojan Horse. Allow others ample liberty while you persistently trot along your chosen path without compro-mising. Success awaits at the end of the trail. The Horse is a free spirit.

Those born during a Horse Year are passionate in love, enthusiastic, inde-pendent, optimistic, and quite strong, both physically and intellectually. They do have a tinge of selfishness though, and can be quick-tempered. If you were born in a Horse year, prance forward confidently. It's your time to race to victory. A cherished wish is fulfilled; enjoy a reward and cultivate promising opportunities. Chinese New Year commences with the second New Moon after the winter solstice, in late January to mid-February.

Years of the Horse
1918, 1930, 1942, 1954, 1966, 1978, 1990, 2002, 2014

More information on the Wood Horse can be found on our website at http://The WitchesAlmanac.com/AlmanacExtras/.

Illustration by Ogmios MacMerlin

sagittarius
November 22 – December 20
Mutable Sign of Fire △ Ruled by Jupiter ♃

S	M	T	W	T	F	S
RUIS (ELDER)						Nov. 22
Scandinavian legends tell of the Elder Mother who watches for any injury to the tree. If even a sprig is cut without first asking permission of the Elder Mother, whatever purpose the sprig is cut for will end in misfortune. Once permission (continued below)						Sagittarius
23 WAXING	24 Time for a new start	25 Andrew Carnegie born, 1835 Capricorn	26	27 Beware of lightning Aquarius	28	29 Pisces
30	Dec. 1 Aries	2 Listen to your familiars	3 Save coins Taurus	4	5 Enchant a love Gemini	6 Oak Moon
7 WANING	8 Pray to Diana Cancer	9 Junior Wells born, 1934	10 Leo	11 Light candles	12	13 Virgo
14	15 Polish copper Libra	16 Fairy Queen Eve	17 Saturnalia Scorpio	18	19 Sagittarius	20

has been asked and a twig of the elder secured, it will banish evil spirits and may be hung or worn as an amulet. Elder flowers, dried while the moon waxes from dark to full, are a potent love charm. The berries gathered at summer solstice afford protection from all unexpected dangers, including accidents and lightning strikes. — excerpt from *Celtic Tree Magic*

THE MIGHTY OAK

THE OAK has long been held sacred, an awe reflected in the prodigious and impressive height reached by the species. An average life span runs to 250 years, but some oaks in England's Windsor Great Park are over a thousand years old. Depending on the variety, the trees range in height from 40 to 120 feet. The leaf form varies, but all oaks bear acorns.

Tales of many ancient European tribes reveal the belief that the oak was the first tree to be created. The Greeks dedicated it to Zeus, and his oracle at Dodona served in an oak grove. Under a great tree a priestess interpreted rustles of the leaves in answer to questions posed by supplicants. Romans believed the oak belonged to the great god Jupiter, and its leaves were a badge of honor. Oak leaves and acorns formed wedding wreaths to assure fertility. The Teutonic and Scandinavian tribes associated the oak with Thor, god of thunder. Boughs of oak protected home and barn from lightning strikes. Celtic Druids, priests of Gaul and Britain, from whom much of witchcraft's lore and legend derives, so revered the oak tree that their teaching and many spiritual rites were performed in its shade. The essential veneration may be traced to the fact that the acorn, fruit of the oak, was once a major food source to the wandering tribes of prehistoric Europe.

But look at the tree itself. Its giant twisted form reveals a brooding mystery. The way the branches reach out, turn and thrust against the sky shows it to be the tree a mystic mind would choose as its own. And the acorn in magical lore symbolizes the highest form of fertility – creativity of the mind.

capricorn
December 21 – January 19
Cardinal Sign of Earth ♀ Ruled by Saturn ♄

S	M	T	W	T	F	S
DEC. 21 ● Capricorn	22 ⇐Winter Solstice ❄	23 WAXING	24 Kiss under mistletoe Aquarius	25	26 Hold a ghost's hand Pisces	27 Louis Pasteur born, 1822
28 ◑ Aries	29	30 Make an earth charm Taurus	31	JAN. 1 2015	2 Feed the birds Gemini	3
4 (Wolf Moon) Cancer	5 WANING	6 Abandon old habits Leo	7	8 Eat sunflower seeds	9 Feast of Janus Virgo	10
11 Libra	12 Snow!	13 ◐	14 Light a fire outdoors Scorpio	15	16 Slow down Sagittarius	17
18 John Partridge born, 1644 Capricorn	19					

BETH (BIRCH)

Few trees figure more prominently in the folklore of Northern Europe than the birch. Deemed sacred to Thor, Norse god of thunder and lightning, the birch symbolizes youth and springtime. It is one of the hardiest trees in the world; growing further north, and, with the rowan and the ash, higher up mountains than any other species. The birch is called "the tree of inception" with good reason. Not only does it self-sow, forming groves, but it is one of the earliest forest trees to put out leaves in spring.

— excerpt from *Celtic Tree Magic*

Notable Quotations
THE EARTH

And forget not that the earth delights to feel your bare feet and the winds long to play with your hair.

– Khalil Gibran

It suddenly struck me that that tiny pea, pretty and blue, was the Earth. I put up my thumb and shut one eye, and my thumb blotted out the planet Earth. I didn't feel like a giant. I felt very, very small.

– Neil Armstrong

The true object of all human life is play. Earth is a task garden; heaven is a playground.

– Gilbert K. Chesterton

Earth laughs in flowers.

– Ralph Waldo Emerson

Earth and sky, woods and fields, lakes and rivers, the mountain and the sea, are excellent schoolmasters, and teach some of us more than we can ever learn from books.

– John Lubbock

The earth is the mother of all people, and all people should have equal rights upon it.

– Chief Joseph

Shall I not have intelligence with the earth? Am I not partly leaves and vegetable mould myself.

– Henry David Thoreau

Trees are the earth's endless effort to speak to the listening heaven.

– Rabindranath Tagore

The longer one is alone, the easier it is to hear the song of the earth.

– Robert Anton Wilson

Quotes compiled by Isabel Kunkle.

aquarius

January 20 – February 18

Fixed Sign of Air ♎ Ruled by Uranus ⛢

S	M	T	W	T	F	S
		Jan. 20 Aquarius	21 Year of the Sheep WAXING	22 Pisces	23	24 Aries
25	26 Taurus	27	28 *Jackson Pollock born, 1912*	29 Gemini	30	31 *Gather falling snow* Cancer
Feb. 1 Oimelc Eve	2 Candlemas	3 Storm Moon Leo	4 WANING	5 Virgo	6 *Visit a frozen pond*	7
8 Libra	9 *Talk with a friend*	10 Scorpio	11	12 Sagittarius	13	14 *Magic Sam born, 1937*
15 Lupercalia Capricorn	16 *Cast a spell*	17 Aquarius	18			

LUIS (ROWAN)

Rowan figures prominently in Scottish folklore as a sure means to counteract evil intent. It was believed that a christened person need only touch a suspected witch with rowan wood in order to break a spell as the poet Alan Ramsay wrote: "Rowan tree and red thread, will put witches to their speed." Yet, a century earlier, in the case of Margaret Barclay, such a charm was damning evidence. Brought to trial for witchcraft in the town of Irvine, Ayrshire, Scotland in 1618, her conviction was assured when a piece of rowan tied with red yarn was found in her possession. – excerpt from *Celtic Tree Magic*

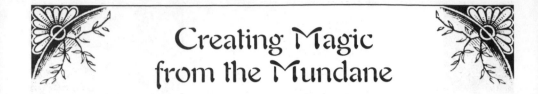

Creating Magic
from the Mundane

BENEATH Mother Earth's surface, there lies a magical world of macro- and micro-organisms that enables life to exist. Although we may love our Mother Earth and do our best to do no harm, this is no longer enough. We need to be more proactive in helping to strengthen and enhance the planet. Just by adding one more step to our pre-existing rituals, we can nourish our deeply depleted planet.

A step easily incorporated into our regular rituals is to take the ashes from our bonfires, Yule logs, and funeral pyres to add to our gardens, shrubs, and fruit trees. Ash adds potassium to our soil, which will enhance the blooming and fruiting process of plants and trees.

Another mundane chore easily transformed into an earth-enhancing ritual is the laborious task of cutting grass. Mowing the lawn can be very meditative and provides a wonderful opportunity to work on mantras for transformation. All the clippings created are high in nitrogen, which is essential to the growth of all things green. If clippings are short, they may be left in place to enhance the lawn. Alternatively, clippings may be used to mulch herbs and leafy vegetables, like spinach, kale, lettuce, and collards. Not only will you be attaining self transformation, but your grass will be

transformed into a manicured lawn and your garden into a show place.

Keep this in mind when raking in the fall. If you have blueberries, azaleas, or rhododendrons, mulch them with pine needles removed from the lawn. These needles raise the acidity of the soil, enabling acid loving shrubs to thrive. Leaves can also be used as mulch or to enhance compost.

By extending our rituals and giving back to Earth, we expand our magic, which can touch more facets of our lives and imbue itself into the plants we grow and eat. Eventually, we will consume these plants as food or medicine and complete the magical circle started months prior. Not only does this extension of our magical work enhance the earth and all it contains, it is also frugal and keeps the planet greener by replacing synthetic fertilizers with our powerful intentions.

Even that which is considered mundane can be transformed into a powerful ritual that enhances our lives, our health, and our planet. The only thing necessary is the desire to bring magic into every aspect of our daily lives. When this is achieved, we will nourish ourselves on all levels: body, mind, and spirit.

– LINDA PATTERSON

pisces

February 19 – March 20

Mutable Sign of Water ▽ Ruled by Neptune ♆

S	M	T	W	T	F	S
NION (ASH) The Greeks dedicated the ash tree to Poseidon, god of the sea, and sailors carried its wood as protection against the threat of drowning. *(continued below)*				FEB. 19 Year of the Horse WAXING Pisces	20	21 Aries
22	23 Taurus	24	25 Gemini	26	27 Love with passion	28 Zero Mostel born, 1915 Cancer
MARCH 1 Matronalia	2 Shed a tear Leo	3	4 Look for the moon's ring Virgo	5 Chaste Moon	6 WANING	7 Libra
8	9 Mircea Eliade born, 1907 Scorpio	10	11 Read a book	12 Sagittarius	13	14 Capricorn
15 Daylight Savings Time begins @ 2am	16 Aquarius	17	18 Minerva's Day ⇨ Pisces	19 Total solar eclipse ⇨	20	

The major spiritual significance of the ash tree comes from Northern Europe, where as Yggdrasil, the World Tree, it connects the underworld, earth and heaven. The ash is associated in Norse myths with Odin (Woden), supreme among gods, who sought to increase his wisdom with extreme suffering. It was on an ash tree that he hanged himself. – excerpt from *Celtic Tree Magic*

Scheherazade

Talking, talking for dear life

THE ARABIAN NIGHTS hurls its whirling text into existence on a "frame story," an ancient narrative device. In this case a Persian king discovers that his new bride has been sexually lively during his absences. King Shahyar roars with rage and orders the queen beheaded, along with her guilty partners. Now loathing all women, the king marries a virgin each night and has her executed each morning. Since shedding blood seems to be royal sport, according to stories everywhere, this goes on until three thousand maidens have lost their heads. Such a horrifying practice brings out a community crisis, as presently it suffers a serious shortage of maidens.

Marriage-and-murder events are arranged by the vizier, literally "burden bearer," the high minister. His beautiful

daughter Scheherazade offers herself as the next sacrifice; the vizier reluctantly agrees. But she has a secret scheme to save herself and other young women. On their wedding night Scheherazade begins to tell the king a long exciting story. As the plot reaches its climax, the queen tells the king that she can only continue the following night, since dawn is breaking. Enormously enter-  tained, King Shahyar agrees. The artful storyteller does finish the story the following night, but immediately begins another cliffhanger. Scheherazade keeps the king entertained and eventually becomes his beloved queen. Through the years the beautiful storyteller provides King Shahyar with one-thousand-and-one stories, three sons and a legacy of wisdom.

About everything

According to Sir Richard Burton, the best English translator from the Arabic, stories came from a dazzling variety of sources. She "had perused the books, annals and legends of the preceding Kings, and the stories, examples and instances of bygone men and things; indeed it was said that she had collected a thousand books of histories related to antique races and departed rulers. She

had perused the works of the poets and knew them by heart; she had studied philosophy and the sciences, arts and accomplishments."

The books spring from the frame tale, but many strange things happen to plots through the thickets of narrative forest. Most commonly known as *The Arabian Nights*, the tales vary widely in tone and subject, and digressions pop up everywhere – every encounter has an entertaining story, simple or complex. Stories within stories offer a heady mix of tragedy, comedy, history, farce, felony, adventure, deceit, riches, poverty, poetry. Plenty of love stories and in certain versions plenty of erotica. Magic in abundance, sometimes in the oriental form of wizards and genies.

From everywhere

Moving on to factual sources of the stories, the first reference to *Nights* derives from a ninth-century fragment, popular stories transcribed from the oral tradition. A century later a similar book of composite tales exists, known in India and Greece as the Persian *A Thousand Tales*, added to haphazardly over time. Shortly thereafter a Persian writer begins an actual collection of one thousand tales, but dies in 942 after

only four hundred eighty are compiled. The "thousand tales" expression may not have been literal, but a buzz term for any large number. The final Eastern version appears in the sixteenth century, earlier tales supplemented by Islamic Crusade accounts and more tales brought to the Middle East by the Mongols.

The first European edition came out in France, twelve volumes published by Galland early in the eighteenth century. Some of the most famous *Nights* stories, while based on Arabic fables, were published first in the French edition – *Aladdin's Wonderful Lamp*, *Ali Baba and the Forty Thieves*, and *The Seven Voyages of Sinbad the Sailor*. Other versions followed in various numbers of volumes and various languages, including English, until Sir Richard Burton got to work and produced his *Arabian Nights* in 1885 – long the gold-standard English translation of Scheherazade's wondrous stories.

Sir Richard Burton, living legend

Burton's life itself sounds like a tale from the teeming brain of Scheherazade. He was a brilliant scholar as well as a man of action – traveler, adventurer, explorer, daredevil. He had a mind-boggling grasp of languages and could speak twenty-five European, Asian and African languages, with dialects that brought the number to forty. This is not a fictional accounting.

Born in England in 1821, Burton was the son of a military officer who chose to raise his children in France and Italy. But the European upbringing left Burton shaky about his English identity. He considered himself "a waif, a stray… a blaze of light without a focus." He was expelled from Oxford over a trivial prank and showed his displeasure in a farewell gesture, trampling college flower beds with horse and carriage.

Burton joined the Army and served in India for the next eight years. "I am fit for nothing more than to be shot at for sixpence a day," he wrote. "Ruffian Dick" Burton was as notable for battle ferocity as for eccentricity. During his time as a soldier he kept a large menagerie of tame monkeys, hoping to access their language. Meanwhile Burton had learned Arabic, Hindi, Marathi, Sindhi, Pashto, Punjabi, Telugu and Multani. His most famous accomplishment was effecting a *hajj*, a well-documented pilgrimage to Mecca, forbidden to outsiders. Burton prepared himself by traveling disguised among Muslims and devoting himself to the culture, including having himself circumcised to reduce the risk if discovery loomed.

Following his military service Burton was engaged by the Royal Geographic Society to explore Africa, and led an expedition credited with the discovery of Lake Tanganyika. He served as consul to Damascus and Trieste, and was awarded a knighthood by Queen Victoria in 1888.

From sex to Sufi

In addition to the first unexpurgated version of *A Thousand and One Nights*, sixteen volumes with its supplement, Burton achieved fame with his ten-volume translation of the Sanskrit sex manual, the *Kama Sutra*. The whiffs of erotica were received by the Victorian public with wrinkled noses. But the *Kasidah*, an ecstatic long poem fragrant with subtle Sufi teaching, established Burton's status as a learned Sufi with that community. Incredible as it seems the author published over eighty volumes and wrote over two hundred articles. His scholarship and style dazzle us. But for posterity, the jewel in his literary crown is the marvelous *Arabian Nights*.

Sir Richard Burton died in Trieste in 1890. He was buried with his wife Isabel Arundal at Mortlake, a Catholic cemetery near London, in a mausoleum formed like a tent that features both crescent and cross. Burton had promised his wife that they would rest side by side in a Bedouin tent throughout eternity, and so they do.

– BARBARA STACY

76

Window on the Weather

Weather in lore and science found common ground
through the centuries as explored here. Humanity's
survival has depended on developing weather precepts
through the ages. Now, our emerging understanding of
the atmosphere's physics dovetails into a longer, more
intuitive sense of natural earth cycles. Confirmation of
what had long been considered the exclusive domain
for an exclusive group of seers with innate knowledge
is available for all who possess curiosity for the world
around them. Use the following as a field guide as we
pass through the seasons to come.

– TOM C. LANG

March 2014

When the wind is blowing in the North
No fisherman should set forth,

When the wind is blowing in the
East, 'Tis not fit for man nor beast,

When the wind is blowing in the South
It brings the food over the fish's mouth,

When the wind is blowing in the West,
That is when the fishing's best!

No other month is as renowned for wind as the month of March. A time of great atmospheric energy, storms are common on the West and East Coasts. A single storm can manifest variant wind directions, all producing various precipitation forms, depending on location and direction. Great storms may still bring heavy snow to New England, the Great Lakes, and the Rocky Mountain states. Peril is sensed in the Deep South with the arrival of tornado season and preceded on any given day by a strong south wind. This, however, often signals abundant rain and an end to drought in the nation's heartland.

April 2014

If it thunders on All Fool's day,
It brings good crops of corn and hay.

Such is the hope of farmers across the Midwest, where stories of the great Dust Bowl era have been playing out in recent years. Pacific Ocean forces have wreaked havoc on crops, starved for moisture in such conditions. Those influences are easing and recent rains bode well for a more balanced and hopeful outlook there. Conversely, rainfall has been more abundant in the West; a trend is likely to continue within the current pattern. A cool, damp spring may be expected in the Northeast, bringing stiff east winds and chilly temperatures. The tornado season reaches its peak in the Deep South and heavy snows continue to blanket the Rockies. West Coast storms are confined to Northern California, Oregon, and Washington.

May 2014

A wet spring is a sign of
dry weather for harvest.

No weather pattern lasts forever and whichever one seems fully established during one season is often countervailed by another of equal and opposite force during the months that follow. Thus, a spring that brings seemingly endless rains can lead to abundant crops; conversely, a dry and benign spring can precede a long-lasting summer drought. The former seems most likely for areas east of the Rockies this year. Tornadoes become evident through the Central and Northern Great Plains.

June 2014

Midsummer Day be ever so little rainy,
The hazel and walnut will be scarce;
Corn smitten in many places;
But apples, pears, and plums
will not be hurt.

Shadowy uncertainty lingers, with concerns regarding continued drought across our farmlands. It is best to consider the nature of cycles and trust their consistency. As Santayana observed, "The only constant in nature is repetition." That is certainly true with our climate, where seeming permanent change invariably regresses to a mean pattern, sometimes with great suddenness. We should be heartened by the prospect of that truth, as we enter the summer growing season. Rainfall is likely to be normal for most, with thunderstorms most prevalent in the North. Hot and humid weather is slow to arrive the Deep South this year. Northeast reservoirs will be bank full.

July 2014

Rain in the third hour of a July
afternoon is the heaviest of the year.

Indeed, at least for most of the United States, it is afternoon and evening summer thunderstorms that bring the most intense rainfall in the shortest time span. This is true in the North, where occasional cold fronts advance from Canada. So too, torrential downpours descend from sea breeze-induced convective storms in Florida and those arising from southeast trade winds in the Carolinas and Georgia. Occasionally, winds are strong, although July tornadoes are relatively rare. Monsoon rains arrive daily and at approximately the same time in the Rockies, although amounts vary greatly from place to place. Annual rainfall amounts are evident by the type and density of plant and tree life.

August 2014

Dry August and warm,
Doth harvest no harm

Spring and early summer rainfall sets the tone for late summer crop yield. The current patterns favor continued drought relief across the nation's heartland and southern Plains. Meanwhile, the East Coast remains vulnerable to occasional hurricane threats for the next several years, given solar and ocean cycles concerning sunspots and the resulting sea surface temperatures. This pattern is similar to one experienced during the 1950s, a decade that greatly impacted New York City and New England. The West Coast is bathed in golden sunshine and gentle breezes.

September 2014

If the oak bear much mast [acorns]
It foreshows a long and hard winter.

Persistence and the dwell of particular pattern is a fine predictor of what will follow – true with both short- and long-term weather forecasting. Animal and plant life react to current conditions, reflected in behavior and, in the case of some plants, yield output. Meteorologically, data provides us with insight and suggests that a cold winter follows a combined chilly September and October about two thirds of the time. In accordance with the adaptive laws of nature, an abundance of acorns would, for example, provide for a lengthy winter encountered by squirrels. Balancing warm weather in the recent past, odds favor a cool fall this year in the East with continuing vulnerability to tropical storm activity. Conversely, the West trends warm and dry.

October 2014

If the moon show a silver shield,
Be not afraid to reap your field;
But if she rises haloed round,
Soon we'll tread on deluged ground.

To the keen observer, the October sky yields clear signs of pending weather changes. This is based on sound science. A watchful eye may witness a circle around the sun or moon, as a storm approaches. This indicates the advance of moisture from a developing storm, at some distance, with storm clouds and wind soon following. The advance of fall polar air makes this signature more observable than at other times. Abundant crops follow a temperate summer with plentiful rainfall for much of the country. Only California's valleys are a little drier than normal.

November 2014

The moon and the weather
may change together,
But a change of the moon will not
change the weather.

As a matter of coincidental circumstance, weather phenomena may appear within lunar cycles. There is, however, no evidence that those patterns are actually caused by the moon's phases. What can be stated is that certain phases will amplify the effects of certain weather patterns. Such is the case during the first coastal storms of November, when an east wind during the full moon raises the risk of flooding. Conversely, a strong west wind can enhance a low tide at the times of high and low tide. Cold arrives in the central United States leading to early snowfall.

with the annual solar cycle by about a month, with long term averages indicating the coldest time at the end of January in the Northern Hemisphere. The coldest air often is the cleanest and driest, absent particulates and being quite dense. Thus, we witness the enchanting luminosity of a full moon reflecting a still January night's deep snow cover. Powdery snows fall near the Great Lakes, Cape Cod, and North Carolina's Outer Banks as unusual cold arrives. A freeze is possible in Florida and California.

Both coasts enjoy quiet weather with several fast moving but weak storms and normal temperatures. California and Florida enjoys pleasant weather.

December 2014

No weather's ill if the wind be still.

The wind is most gentle during times of high pressure, an occurrence generally bringing fair weather. High pressure tends to be strongest during the winter, much of the North American heartland being dominated by such a weather regime. Yet it is under high pressure that arctic air builds. So, too, the places between high and low pressure, where storms reside, is where winds often howl. The likelihood for that is highest along the Northeast Coast and the Pacific Northwest, where an early winter can occur this year. Snow can fall early in the interior, while the Northern Plains are frigid.

January, 2014

When stars shine clear and bright,
We will have a very cold night.

Days lengthen, yet temperatures fall further through January. The planet's heat balance remains out of phase

February 2015

The winds of the daytime
wrestle and fight,
Longer and stronger
than those of the night

As winter advances and the days lengthen, the sun appears higher in the sky. Its rays are more direct on the earth's surface and, where there is no snow, the wind begins to blow during the day. Winds ease at night with the setting sun and yet a pattern has begun that leads to more tumultuous weather in the South, where thunderstorms become more common as energy becomes available. Overall, more wind energy can accelerate the formation of larger-scale powerful storms. This appears to be most likely along the West Coast this year and, in particular, in Central California and the Rockies. Normal snowfall can be expected in the East.

Straw Men and Scarecrows

When Broonie got a cloak or hood [Brownie]
He did his master nae mair good [no more good]
                                    – Traditional Scottish saying

HARRY POTTER fans will remember how Dobby the house-elf was freed by receiving a gift of clothing. This is actually based on an old Scottish belief that the brownie (a type of helpful spirit), who lives on your land will depart once he or she receives a gift of clothing.

The mundane purpose of a scarecrow is to repel birds and protect the fields, but in order to be magically protective, the scarecrow, like a brownie, should never be dressed. The "straw man" should be made from the last sheaf of the harvest by binding the straw to a wooden framework, and should never be clothed.

Binding straw to a scaffold to make a straw man is more than an artistic or practical act. Preserving and honoring the straw from a previously successful harvest is a way of transferring the luck from one year to the next.

Corn dollies and straw dogs

In Celtic areas, the last sheaf was often made into a "corn dolly" and carefully preserved on the mantle. Straw dolls representing the goddess Bride or Brighid were paraded around the village at Imbolc to bring the blessings of the harvest to every door.

In Orkney and France, a straw dog was made from the last sheaf of the harvest, to be stored and brought out again at Christmas. In very ancient times, it was believed that a she-wolf spirit guarded and nurtured the fields, the crops, and the people, and that the wolf could be seen when ripples of wind moved through the fields. The last sheaf of the harvest was fashioned into a canine figure, because the spirit of the harvest was said to inhabit the last sheaf gathered.

The last sheaf

In other areas of Europe, the last sheaf was made into a mare or a goat but the idea was the same: that an animal spirit was the sacred guardian of the fields and the harvest and that this spirit was magically preserved in the last sheaf to be cut.

In Lithuania, the last European country to be converted to Christianity, a straw bear ceremony was performed on the twelfth day of Christmas. The straw 'bear' was actually a man wrapped in pea plant straw, who was accompanied by another straw-wrapped man. Accompanied by musicians, the 'bear' was led around every house in the village. Every housewife danced with the 'bear' and then gave coins to the performers. As the 'bear' danced through the village, it brought luck, fertility, and the Spirit of the Grain into every home.

In Andorra, the performance involved a bear dressed in a straw coat that was ritually killed and then miraculously jumped out of its own funeral pyre, symbolizing the death and rebirth of the grain in the new planting season.

The harvest rose

Straw, symbol of the luck of the harvest, found its way into other customs. In Germany, a woman or a man was wrapped in straw, marking the end of the harvest. In Orkney, farm hands gave a "harvest rose"– a plaited straw token – to their lovers. In Shetland, weddings were blessed by masked men wearing straw dresses led by a "scudler" with a straw broom. In England and else-where, straw figures are still made as a hobby, to decorate the home. In Germany and Austria, straw is used to fashion Christmas tree decorations and in Sweden, straw goats are featured at Yule.

Kuebiko, a Shinto *kami*, is a spirit of wisdom and agriculture, who is also a scarecrow. Because he stands unmoving in the middle of the field, he is the watcher who sees and knows all things. Kuebiko is the wise spirit who protects the farm.

The next time you make or see a scarecrow, realize that the straw used to make the figure came from a previous year's successful planting. Try to use the last sheaf of the harvest when you make one, so you can build a home for the Spirit of the Grain to bless your farm. Do it to bring the magical fertility of a successful harvest into your home and garden and to transfer the luck from one agricultural cycle to the next.

– ELLEN EVERT HOPMAN

83

The Cimaruta

AMONG THE MANY folk charms of Italy, we find one of particular significance and antiquity. It is commonly known as the cimaruta (pronounced chee-mah-roo-tah). In Italian, the word "cima" means the "top" of something. The word "ruta" translates into the English word for the herb rue. Putting the two words together, we find that cimaruta means the top of the rue plant, which is where the buds and flowers appear.

In Italy, during the 19th century, the cimaruta charm was quite popular. Among the common people it was most often used to protect against "envy" and the "evil eye" (particularly in the case of keeping infants safe). It was a common practice to place a silver cimaruta charm on the crib, and this was often tied with a strip of red wool. The magical power of the cimaruta lies, in part, with the old magical reputation of the rue plant itself.

Traditional uses of the cimaruta
One of the misconceptions about rue is that it is an herb specifically against witchcraft. But this sole assignment is untrue. Rue's reputation is that of an herb used against enchantments, which means its nature is counteractive against magic in general. Since magic is not exclusive to witchcraft we cannot diminish rue to an anti-witchcraft charm.

The traditional cimaruta charm is made of silver and worn as a necklace piece. Most of the antique pieces measure about three inches long and two inches wide. The charm is fashioned in the design of a sprig of rue divided into its three primary branches. Each branch terminates into a bud from which is suspended a symbolic charm. These charms differ depending upon from which region in Italy the specific cimaruta piece originated.

A similar Iberian charm
In Spain and Portugal we find a similar charm suggestive of a folkloric tradition behind the cimaruta that was more widespread than just throughout Italy. The charm is known as *cinco seimao*, and is comprised of five symbols: a pentagram, a figa hand, a human-faced crescent, and a key, all of which are grouped around a heart pierced by two arrows. Standing on top of the heart is the image of what commentators describe as the Virgin Mary. Of interest is the appearance of a flower on the wrist of the figa hand, which also appears on the cimaruta as a separate charm. Folklorist W.L. Hildburgh comments:

In the cinco seimao *we find combined the protective virtues of silver, of an image of the Virgin, of the lunar crescent, the key, the ithyphallic hand, the heart, and the pentagram, and possibly also those of the flower-like emblem, the arrow, and the cross. In the Neapolitan cimaruta we find embodied several of the same conceptions which are embraced by the* cinco seimao. *The cimaruta, literally the "sprig of rue," is a stem from which extend short branches, each of which holds an amuletic emblem or symbol at its extremity. It is worn as a protection against* Jetiatura *(the evil eye), it is almost always of silver, and usually roughly made, and it counts amongst its symbols the lunar crescent, the key, the ithyphallic hand (the* mano fica*), a flower-like emblem, and often the heart and the arrow. The number of coincidences between the two amulets appears too great to be the result of mere chance; in fact it is so great that we may fairly assume that the amulets themselves have had a common origin, and that one or the other has changed in form, and in some of its less valued symbols, during the centuries since their genesis.*

Protection of infants
Most of what is publicly known of the cimaruta comes from various writings of the late 19th century and early 20th century. Almost without exception the majority of writers of this period associate the cimaruta with the protection of infants. As previously mentioned in this article, protection involved hanging the charm on the crib of the infant. An additional practice was to fix garlic to the infant's chest and sprinkle rue around the mother's bed. Such practices arose as a protection against envy, which was viewed as a sinister force. The fear being that people visiting the newborn infant and its mother might be envious, which would contaminate the child and draw vitality away from its life force.

Some writers of the 19th century appear to be aware of the cimaruta as a charm of pagan origin associated with the goddess Diana and with witchcraft. This is supported through old oral teachings preserved among some practitioners of Italian witchcraft. Here we learn that the cimaruta contains lunar symbolism directly linked to the goddess of witchcraft. According to this lore, witches wear the charm as a token of their devotion to the triformis goddess of witchcraft. It is also worn by witches as a sign to others of their membership in her society. The association of Hecate-Diana-Proserpina with witchcraft is a long-standing tradition in pre-Christian literature.

Hecate – Diana – Proserpina
In ancient writings witches call upon Diana to aid their magic. The Roman poet Horace writes in his *Epodes* that Diana witnesses the deeds of witches in the night. He goes on to say she is the mistress of the silent hour when mystic rites are performed (*Epode 5, verse 50*). Other writings list Diana in a

triformis group with Hecate and Proserpina. One example appears in the works of Apollodorus whose opinion is that Hecate, Diana and Proserpina are all one and the same. Here the triple goddess is described as Hecate in the heavens (the moon), Diana on Earth, and Proserpina in the Underworld.

The beliefs connected to the cimaruta as they appear in common folk magic (protection of the infant) and that of witchcraft (connection to the goddess Diana) seem to not match, but this is due to a surface understanding. In ancient times the goddess Diana played an important role related to pregnant women and birthing. Her sanctuary at Lake Nemi was the site of an annual pilgrimage where women petitioned Diana for a safe and easy labor. Author Eustace Neville Rolfe, in his book *Naples in 1888*, wrote about the cimaruta in connection with Diana and infants.

Diana, Queen of Heaven

Rolfe writes that in her aspect of Diana Pronuba, the goddess oversaw maternity. Concerning rue, the author states "the rue plant is the herb of maternity, and clearly represents Diana Pronuba, while the key represents Diana Jana, the heart Diana Virgo, and the moon the Queen of Heaven." Folklorist Frederick Elworthy, in his book *The Evil Eye,* remarks that three branches of rue represent Diana Triformis or her prototype. He equates Diana with Proserpina who he states is concerned for women in labor. Rolfe writes in conclusion:

Of all the many charms combined in the Cimaruta we find on close study that there is scarcely one which may not directly or indirectly be considered as connected with Diana, the goddess of infants, worshipped today by Neapolitans as zealously as ever she was in old times by the men of Ephesus and Rome; the only change is in her name. Many a Demetrius, who still makes her silver shrines, flourishes near the Piazza Margherita, though nowadays he knows her only as La Madonna; she is, however, his goddess, his 'regina del Cielo, della terra, del parto, ed anche del inferno.'

Thus far we have seen that the amulet contains no directly Christian emblem. There is no trace in it of a cross, a halo, a crown, or a palm branch. None of the emblems which we habitually see in the ancient catacombs, or in the modern churches, are discernible, and both catacombs and churches are accustomed to display symbols of various kinds with astonishing prodigality. We must consequently conclude that, after something like sixteen centuries of Christianity, an amulet exists in Italy in which heathen emblems only prevail. There is, in fact, nothing we can twist into a Christian symbol, excepting so far only as the worship

of the Virgin Mary at Naples today is identical with, and a survival of, the worship of Diana Tifatina at Capua in the Roman times.

Symbols of the cimaruta

Despite the obvious intimate connection of the cimaruta with pre-Christian symbolism, most modern scholars insist upon its use in Christian culture as an indication of its meaning (if not origin). As noted earlier, the cimaruta is regarded by modern academics as strictly an anti-witch charm used by superstitious Catholic peasants in 19th century Italy. However, when we examine the symbolism of the cimaruta it becomes difficult to understand how it meshes with Catholic beliefs in such a way that the charm reflects Christian tenets. We should expect to find only Christian symbolism in a charm designed to protect the Catholics of Italy who relied upon it. But in its earliest forms such symbols do not exist. In order to understand the cimaruta as a non-Catholic devise used by witches we must revisit the symbolism and see them through the eyes of the witch.

As we have seen, the 19th century cimaruta charm was most commonly comprised of several symbols that readily identified it. These were attached to the sprig of rue plant design, encircling it to form one complete amulet. All cimaruta pieces of this era contained the following symbols: hand, moon, key, flower, horn or dagger, rooster (or sometimes an eagle), and the serpent. Later other symbols were added to the cimaruta. Among the most common were the heart, the cornucopia, and the cherub angel. The later addition of the heart (sometimes depicted as a flaming heart) and the cherub are the only ones to reflect Catholic theology. When we compare this cimaruta design with earlier ones, the heart or the cherub is always placed in areas that are empty spaces in the earlier cimaruta piece designs. What does that suggest?

The triformis goddess of witchcraft

As noted earlier in the article, the branches of the rue naturally divide into three trunks. This we can regard as being representative of a triple nature, and therefore it can be connected with the triformis goddess of witchcraft. Most scholars argue that the concept of a triple goddess associated with witches or witchcraft is an entirely modern notion. But this is incorrect.

The Roman poet Ovid (in his work titled *Metamorphoses*) mentions "the sacred rites of the three-fold goddess" in connection to an oath sworn to the witch Medea, and portrays her as a priestess of the goddess Hecate. Lucan writes (in Book 6 of his *Bellum Civile*) of witches worshipping Hecate as a triformis goddess, with Persephone being the "lowest of the three aspects." The Roman poet Catullus writes of Diana as a "three-fold" goddess, and Horace associates witches with the goddess Diana who watches over their rites. Virgil refers to Diana as having three faces and names one as Hecate. Horace writes that witches worship Hecate, Diana, and Proserpina (Persephone). An Orphic tradition also joined Hecate, Diana, and Persephone (Proserpina) into one triformis goddess. None of this is proof that witches actually worshipped a triformis goddess in ancient times, but it is proof that the concept itself is not a modern invention.

Diana's dart

One of the titles for Diana is Queen of the Fairies, and in accord with this the vervain blossom on the cimaruta gains even greater significance through its faery connection. The relevance of the moon is obvious, but in connection with the moon the appearance of the dagger requires further explanation. The dagger represents a moonbeam, the light of Diana directed as she wills. In this context it is known as the dart or arrow of Diana. With it, Diana bestows either enlightenment or lunacy – what a person is prepared on unprepared to receive beneath her emanation of mystical light.

Hecate has been associated with witches and witchcraft almost since her first appearance in ancient writings. Legends about her place Hecate as a goddess who rules over the crossroads. Since ancient times this site has been sacred and magical. An ancient common belief is that the dead who were unable to pass into the Otherworld gathered at the crossroads. Here they came under the protection of Hecate. The key became a very important symbol related to Hecate, because she is the gatekeeper between the worlds. In this light, the key is an important symbol on the cimaruta. However, it is also a sign that the wearer (as a witch) is one to whom no mystery is ever closed.

No stronger symbol of allegiance

The last aspect of the triformis goddess is Proserpina, a mystical form of Persephone. Her name is related to the serpent, which is one of the manifestations in which she presents herself. The serpent is a creature that moves below and above the earth. It passes through the portals between the realms. In this regard the serpent knows the secrets of the Underworld and is a messenger between the living and the dead. On the cimaruta, the serpent moves along the edge of the crescent, symbolizing its connections to the phases of the moon in a mystical shedding of its skin.

As a triformis goddess on the cimaruta, Diana resides in the night sky. Proserpina walks in the Underworld, and Hecate appears in the middle, here on Earth where she stands at the crossroads between the worlds. There can no stronger symbol of allegiance to the Triformis Goddess, and to the way of witchcraft, than the cimaruta charm.

– RAVEN GRIMASSI
Excerpt from *The Cimaruta: and Other Magical Charms from Old Italy*

Atlas in Starry Affliction

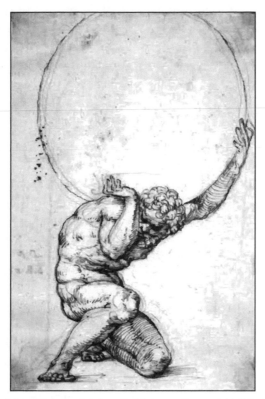

Crouching Figure of Atlas, Baldassare Peruzzi (1481–1536)

PEOPLE STRESSED OUT and overburdened may be haunted by Atlas, for the Greek god held aloft the heavens, "shuddering and shifting the weight upon his trembling shoulders." A Titan fighting on the losing side of the giants' battles with Zeus, his burdens are the thunder god's punishment. The hero Heracles, questing for the Golden Apples of Hesperides, seeks the aid of Atlas, for the magical fruit is guarded by the Titan's starry daughters, the Pleiades. But Heracles will have to hold the vault of the sky while Atlas performs the task. Heracles sustains the burden, but when Alas returns with the apples he refuses to resume the celestial globe. Heracles groans at his ill fortune and pleads for some cushions to pad the strain on his aching shoulders. Atlas, more brawn than brain, lifts the globe to place the pillows, Hercules slips away with the golden prizes, and Atlas again quivers under his starry affliction.

Persephone.

by Jean Ingelow

She stepped upon Sicilian grass,
Demeter's daughter fresh and fair,
A child of light, a radiant lass,
And gamesome as the morning air.
The daffodils were fair to see,
They nodded lightly on the lea,
Persephone – Persephone!

Lo! one she marked of rarer growth
Than orchis or anemone;
For it the maiden left them both,
And parted from her company.
Drawn nigh she deemed it fairer still,
And stooped to gather by the rill
The daffodil, the daffodil.

What ailed the meadow
that it shook?
What ailed the air of Sicily?
She wondered by the brattling brook,
And trembled with the trembling lea.
"The coal-black horses rise – they rise:
O mother, mother!" low she cries –
Persephone – Persephone!

"O light, light, light!"
she cries, "farewell;
The coal-black horses wait for me.
O shade of shades, where I must dwell,
Demeter, mother, far from thee!
Ah, fated doom that I fulfil!
Ah, fateful flower beside the rill!
The daffodil, the daffodil!"

What ails her that she
comes not home?
Demeter seeks her far and wide,
And gloomy-browed
doth ceaseless roam
From many a morn till eventide.
"My life, immortal though it be,
Is nought," she cries, "for want of thee,
Persephone – Persephone!

"Meadows of Enna, let the rain
No longer drop to feed your rills,
Nor dew refresh the fields again,
With all their nodding daffodils!
Fade, fade and droop, O lilied lea,
Where thou, dear heart,
wert reft from me –
Persephone – Persephone!"

She reigns upon her dusky throne,
Mid shades of heroes dread to see;
Among the dead she breathes alone,
Persephone – Persephone!
Or seated on the Elysian hill
She dreams of earthly daylight still,
And murmurs of the daffodil.

A voice in Hades soundeth clear,
The shadows mourn and fill below;
It cries –
"Thou Lord of Hades, hear,
And let Demeter's daughter go.
The tender corn upon the lea

Droops in her goddess
gloom when she
Cries for her lost Persephone.

"From land to land she raging flies,
The green fruit falleth in her wake,
And harvest fields beneath her eyes
To earth the grain unripened shake.
Arise, and set the maiden free;
Why should the world
such sorrow dree
By reason of Persephone?"

He takes the cleft
pomegranate seeds:
"Love, eat with me this parting day;"
Then bids them fetch
the coal-black steeds –
"Demeter's daughter, wouldst away?"
The gates of Hades set her free:
"She will return full soon," saith he –
"My wife, my wife Persephone."

Low laughs the dark king
on his throne –
"I gave her of pomegranate seeds."
Demeter's daughter stands alone
Upon the fair Eleusian meads.
Her mother meets her.
"Hail!" saith she;
"And doth our daylight dazzle thee,
My love, my child Persephone?

"What moved thee,
daughter, to forsake
Thy fellow-maids that fatal morn,
And give thy dark lord power to take
Thee living to his realm forlorn?"
Her lips reply without her will,
As one addressed
who slumbereth still,
"The daffodil, the daffodil!"

Her eyelids droop
with light oppressed,
And sunny wafts that round her stir,
Her cheek upon her mother's breast –
Demeter's kisses comfort her.
Calm Queen of Hades, art thou she
Who stepped so lightly on the lea –
Persephone, Persephone?

When, in her destined
course, the moon
Meets the deep shadow of this world,
And laboring on doth seem to swoon
Through awful wastes
of dimness whirled –
Emerged at length, no trace hath she
Of that dark hour of destiny,
Still silvery sweet – Persephone.

The greater world may near the less,
And draw it through her
weltering shade,
But not one biding trace impress
Of all the darkness that she made;
The greater soul that draweth thee
Hath left his shadow plain to see
On thy fair face, Persephone!

Demeter sighs, but sure 'tis well
The wife should love her destiny:
They part, and yet, as legends tell,
She mourns her lost Persephone;
While chant the maids of Enna still –
"O fateful flower beside the rill –
The daffodil, the daffodil!"

Druid Wands

I have been in the battle of Godeu,
with Lleu and Gwydion,
They changed the forms of
elementary trees and sedges.

– Battle of the Trees, *sung by Taliesin*

A DRUID wielding his magic wand is among history's most powerful, romantic, and persistent images. The Druids were forcibly disbanded and all but annihilated over one-thousand years ago, yet their power still resides within humanity's collective unconscious. It's ironic, considering how little we truly know of them. The Druids were a powerful, priestly class in Celtic society, second only to nobility. Each individual Druid functioned as a priest, diviner, magician, poet, teacher, physician, or legal administrator. They earned their status after a rigorous course of training and memorization that took as many as twenty years to complete. Because they provided religious, civic, academic, divinatory and other magical functions, the Druids were among the first targeted for destruction by the Roman Empire during their conquest of Celtic territory.

Words of their enemies

Even though the Gaulish Druids possessed a system of writing, their beliefs dictated that their mysteries could not be written down. As a result, much of what we know of the Druids comes from outsiders, who were often their enemies.

It seems that the Druids believed trees conveyed their properties to the wands made from them. Trees were categorized into four classes: noble, commoner, shrub, or bramble. Brehon law tracts include the amounts of restitution due for cutting a tree. In some cases, cutting a tree could carry the same penalty as killing a human chief: *A danger from which there is no escape is the penalty for felling the sacred tree, Thou shalt not cut a sacred tree and escape with the fines for the seven noble trees.*

W. Winwood Reade, in his book, *Mysteries of the Druids*, identifies one class as a herald which carries a wand of vervain, "encircled by two serpents." In that same procession, another Druid bears a white wand and the arch druid, a scepter. The very name "Druid" stems from two old Celtic words: *derwos*, meaning "tree," "oak," and "truth" and *vid* or *wid*, meaning "to know." Thus, "Druid" may be interpreted to mean something like "tree knower" or "knower of the oak." Many of the Celtic tribes of Gaul took their names from many kinds of trees, not just oak. Ireland boasted "five great trees" – three types of ash, an oak, and a yew.

The silver bough with golden apples

Tacitus reported that Druids always carried their wands with them. According to Pliny the Elder, "They chose groves formed of oaks for the sake of the tree alone, and they never perform any of their rites except in presence of a branch from it…" It takes but a small leap from modern perceptions of the "wand" to "a branch from" the tree. Among the most notable of these branches in Celtic mythology is the silver apple bough which, when it appears in tales, is inevitably in blossom, laden with golden apples, strung with tinkling bells, or some combination thereof. The silver branch lulled people to sleep when shaken and its sweet music made listeners forget their wants and sorrows.

This silver bough served as a key to the Otherworld which, in his groundbreaking book *The Fairy Faith in Celtic Countries*, author W. Y. Evans-Wentz suggests could be the Celtic ancestral world of the dead. Thus a guide possessing the silver branch was a psychopomp – a conductor of souls between worlds. These journeys were dangerous, as, if something went wrong, the mortal might be left fatally stranded. Evans-Wentz thought this experience could be symbolic of Druidic initiations. His theory is further supported in *The Dialogue of Two Sages*, which describes how Neidh, a young, ambitious bard, who sought to become an arch-poet "made his journey with a silver branch over him."

Wands of Manannan mac Lir

In *The Voyage of Bran, Son of Febal*, the silver branch was born from a fairy woman and Manannan mac Lir, the sea god. In another tale, *Oisin in Tir na Nóg*, a homesick Irish warrior returns to his homeland centuries after he left with the aid of a mystical apple branch. He falls from his horse and, upon touching the ground, instantly ages into an old man. Another story, *Cormac's Adventure in the Land of Promise* culminates with Manannan loaning Cormac the use of the apple branch for the rest of his life. As Manannan had tested him by taking away his family members, one at a time, there is no doubt Cormac had earned it.

Baile and Ailinn

The Celtic view of trees is inherent within the story of Baile and Ailinn, two lovers who died upon hearing they would not meet again in their lifetime. From Ailinn's grave grew an apple tree and, in another province where Baile was laid to rest, a yew. Eventually the trees were both cut down. A wand was cut from each tree and inscribed with a love poem. Two centuries later, the wands chanced to be under the same roof for the first time since the lovers were parted. They flew together, clinging so tightly they couldn't be parted – and so they stayed. Knowing Druids believed in reincarnation, the above story broadens one's mind to the forms in which a Celt could reincarnate. It's no secret that much Druidic wisdom survived and was passed to us through folk belief. A curious belief surrounds the elder tree, also known as the Ellhorn. It states that, before cutting its wood, permission must be sought on bended knee, uttering this charm:

Lady Ellhorn, give me of thy wood,
and I will give thee of mine,
when I become a tree.

The results of wielding a wand were often sensational. They gave Druids the power to focus forces of nature, hush the sounds of battle, bring night when it should be day, raise storms, call up dense fog, drive someone insane, take away an enemy army's courage, confer invisibility, and even determine if someone is a virgin.

Transmogrification

The most commonly seen use of a wand in Celtic myth is in transmogrification, the act of transforming one form into another. For the transformation to occur, the Druid had to touch the wand to the object being transformed, typically a person. We see it in stories such as *The Children of Lir, The Fate of the Children of Tuirean* and *Math, the Son of Mathonwy*. In some stories, we know what type of wand was used. A hazel wand was used to transform Etain into a fly. A handful of straw was thrown at Prince Comgan, cursing him with boils and ulcers and making him insane. Yew, the tree of mystery, was often used to divine hidden things. The Druid Dalan used yew to find Etain after she'd been kidnapped by her husband from a former incarnation. Hazel is still preferred for a divining rod. In a few instances, a wand may be burned to achieve one's goals. For instance, to divine an enemy's location, Druids burnt mountain ash. In another example, Mogh Ruith, the legendary blind Druid, also burned mountain ash, which together with charms served to transform three men into stone. Traditional Bride's Eve celebrations featured a grain doll representing the goddess Bride. The doll was laid in a cradle and placed in the fireplace to divine the coming year. Beforehand, a white wand was bestowed upon her and laid at her side. The next morning, the coming year is divined based on the form of the wand's ashes.

A "branch" as a tool to focus and extend one's reach could have descended to us in many forms – as a magic wand, staff, club, rod, spear, mace, scepter, slat, caduceus, measuring stick, divining rod, key, music conductor's baton, switch, or riding crop. In fact, the wand was a unit of measurement in Pre-Norman England, hearkening back to days when measurements were based on body parts. A wand measured a "yard and a hand" or 1,007 millimeters.

Wending wands

The word "wand" stems from Old Norse *vondr* meaning a supple rod or switch, related to the English word "wend," which means to pursue or direct. The 17th century was the last century when the white wand of sovereignty was ritually bestowed upon a Gaelic king, the King of Ireland. A few obscure poems exist that many feel are remnants of Druid lore as well. Perhaps as a pneumonic device, the Welsh poem, *Cad Goddeu* (*the Battle of the Trees*), could have been used to relate to the different properties of trees. *Buile Suibhne* (*the Madness of Suibhne*) is an Irish poem that may have had a similar use. The *slat an droichta* or Druid's Wand was generally composed of wood or metal and decorated with symbols, animals, and events. Spirals were common decorations. Twisted or hooked branches or those with ivy growing around them in spiral seem to have been favored. A wand's color and adornment indicated the bearer's station and authority. For instance, the chief poet carried a golden wand, the second order poets, silver, and all others, bronze.

By truth the earth endures. – Peter Berresford Ellis, *The Druids*

– Nialla niMacha

Mandalas

Sacred symbols to harness the magic within and without

MANDALAS are designs that create spiritual awakening through artistic expression. Usually circular – the word mandala derives from the Sanskrit word for "circle" – they are wonderful instruments for contemplation and to enhance the energy of rituals. Mandala symbolism was intensely studied by psychologist and mystic, Carl Jung. His writings describe the use of mandalas to transform both the inner self and the outer world. Using sacred geometry, a mandala illustrates a natural and ultimate illusion of wholeness.

There are three basic properties in mandala structure. First, the center, which represents the self, the ego, birth, and eternal beginning. The center is the psyche of the individual. Second, symmetry: the path of order in a chaotic universe. Symmetrical patterns restore balance and wellness within the self and the environment. And finally, third: cardinal points. Numerology is employed in the purpose and orientation of the mandala. The number and design of the cardinal points will direct the energy flow of the mandala.

In creating a personal mandala, two or more points are used and a circle is constructed. In astrology the circular horoscope

chart of twelve zodiac signs and houses assume a mandala form. Seven, the heptagon, is especially powerful. Seven draws upon the symbolism of the colors in the rainbow, the chakras, the days of the week, the seven seas, and the notes in the musical scale. The Witches' Wheel of the Year is an octagon, a circle of the eight seasonal festivals or sabbats. In Feng Shui, the *ba'gua* diagram is also an octagonal mandala.

Four, the square, is another popular and powerful number to select in constructing the cardinal points of the mandala. The square suggests stability, accepting responsibility and elaborating upon an already established position. The pentagram, the five-pointed or pentagon shape, is the unique symbol of witchcraft and adapts beautifully to mandala construction. Five is a number symbolizing life and growth. It appears repeatedly in living organisms. The human body, standing with extended limbs and the head upright, traces the five cardinal points of a pentagonal mandala circle.

Oriental carpets, Pennsylvania Dutch hex symbols, the rose windows in cathedrals, shields, heraldic symbols, and yantras are all examples of the mandala concept. All demonstrate the profound universal significance of mandalas.

Drawing a personal mandala and dedicating it to a goal or life passage is one of the most healing and magical experiences the witch can undertake. First, select a number which resonates with you. Draw a perfect circle. Place the cardinal points of your chosen number with dots at equidistance around the perimeter of your circle. Then, proceed to explore mandala magic for yourself by repeating symbols and designs that appeal to you.

– GRANIA LING

Alpheratz

The star of Pegasus and Andromeda, a lady in distress

THE DISTANT backdrop of deep space twinkles with unique cosmic energies. Some stars are glorious and helpful, while others are negative, even sinister. The fixed stars have been important since astrology's earliest days. Fixed is something of a misnomer. The stars do move ever so slightly; however, the distance traveled over a century is barely perceptible.

Alpheratz is a purplish-white double star of the 2nd magnitude located at 14 degrees Aries 26 minutes. It is benevolent, with the overall nature of Venus. A part of two constellations, both Andromeda and Pegasus, Alpheratz has the added distinction of being among the fifty stars catalogued by the Elizabethan astrologer William Lilly in his book *Christian Astrology*. Alpheratz is also noted by the 1st-century astrologer Manilus in his work *Astronomica* where it appeared on the title page in a drawing of the constellation Andromeda.

The legend is that King Cepheus and Queen Cassiopeia of Ethiopia had a beautiful daughter. The proud parents claimed Andromeda was even more beautiful than the sea nymphs. The nymphs complained to their father, Poseidon, who sent a sea monster to ravage the coast. Terrified, Cepheus learned that the only way to save his kingdom was to sacrifice his daughter. Andromeda was chained to a rock and left to the mercy of the monster. A hero, Perseus, had a quick consultation with the parents who agreed that he could marry her if he rescued the situation. Perseus rode through the air on the winged horse Pegasus and turned the sea monster to stone. The wedding soon followed.

The name Alpheratz derives from the Arabic, *Al Surrat al Faras*, or "the horse's navel." Later this transferred to Andromeda's hair or "the head of the woman in chains." Ptolemy, the 2nd-century Greek astronomer, has been credited with making the switch.

When a fixed star conjoins a luminary or planet it will dominate the outcome of events or the path of an individual's destiny. Consider only the conjunction when placing a fixed star in a birth chart, and the orb is just three degrees. Some keywords showing the significance of Alpheratz' influence in the

Natal Horoscope are in the chart below.

Alpheratz will exert a great deal of influence during 2014 – 15. Uranus will be in orb of a conjunction with this fixed star most of the year. The aspect will be strongest when Uranus is at 14 degrees of Aries during April 30 – May 19, 2014; September 26 – October 20, 2014; and again February 20 – March 11, 2015. The total lunar eclipse on October 8, 2014, will also be in very close proximity to Alpheratz. At these times those practicing ritual magic can invoke the myth archetypes of the rescue of Andromeda by Perseus as well as the power of flight through calling upon Pegasus. Magical workings to save those in distress, especially for the sake of love, and travels for the sake of pure and virtuous motives would be favored.

– DIKKI-JO MULLEN

Alpheratz's Influence in Astrology

With the Sun
Honors, favors granted, and assistance from others
(Those born April 1–7 of any year will have Alpheratz conjunct the Sun.)

With the Moon
Energy, good friends, business success, persistence, and wealth

With Mercury
Pioneering work brings prominence; interest in science, religion, philosophy

With Venus
Good health, luck in games of chance, sociable,
pleasant, and a tidy appearance

With Mars
Astute, high energy, success through originality

With Jupiter
Dignity, spiritual growth, good professional networking

With Saturn
Frugal, seeks popularity, domestic harmony,
prone to health problems involving the head

With Uranus
Good speaker, talent in occult studies, honorable,
practical application of inventive ideas

With Neptune
Humane, reformer, charitable, attracted to animals

With Pluto
Interest in big business; good vitality and recuperative powers

The Library at Alexandria

The place of the cure of the soul

IN THE third century BCE, Alexander the Great founded a magnificent city in conquered Egypt. Believing himself the offspring of both Zeus Ammon and Hercules, acclaimed a pharaoh, Alexander built an urban shrine to his godly, royal self. Dead at thirty-two, Alexander never lived to see his "Great Library," finally established by his successor, Ptolemy I Soter. General awareness still prevails about the collection; that it held all knowledge of the pagan world and that all was lost in a fire.

That the library shelves held "all ancient knowledge" was obvious hyperbole. But the legendary collection was certainly vast, generally estimated at 40,000 to 70,000 and sometimes as many as 700,000 or more scrolls; Carl Sagan, in his PBS series *Cosmos* puts the figure at one million.

A royal mandate strewing riches assembled the world's first library collection striving for "universal synthesis," an ancient intimation of Google. Scrolls were bought in quantity from book fairs in Athens and Rhodes, and original works of Plato, Aristotle, and Hippocrates took their places on the racks or in the pigeonholes, protected by linen or leather jackets. Original works of the dramatists Aeschylus, Euripides and Sophocles were purchased at great price. Treasures were sought from all over Greece, Persia, Assyria, India and elsewhere. Books were requisitioned wherever they could be discovered, including ships docking at the bustling Alexandrian port. Sometimes court scribes quickly copied the scrolls, some forged so accurately that the originals were placed in the library and the copies returned to the oblivious owners.

Wherever the sources, all were written on the plentiful papyrus reeds rustling along the Nile, one technology removed from cumbersome stone and clay tablets.

Brains and glory

The Great Library also was conceived as a research institution. If you build it they will come, and come they did. Sometimes as many as one hundred international scholars–researchers, translators, writers, lecturers, copyists and their families – flocked to live at the complex. The colony was well subsidized by successive pharaohs with stipends, housing, travel, community dining and recreation. In addition to archives of ancient learning, the scholars produced new works in mathematics, astrology, astronomy, medicine, philology, physics and the natural sciences. Euclid worked there and so did Archimedes. Poetry was cherished. Library scholars created the first critical studies of Homer and Hesiod, eliminating accumulated dross and redeeming gold. The Greek poet Challimachus was instrumental. A head librarian, he produced the *Pinakes*, the *Lists*, 120 volumes cataloging the complete collection and lost during the Byzantine era.

Of the structures themselves no trace remains, although we know they formed a superb complex adjacent to an earlier edifice, the *Mouseion*, "Temple of the Muses." The *Serapeion*, a nearby daughter museum dedicated to the fertility god Serapis, held a smaller book collection. The Great Library, sited in the Royal Quarters, included an elegant colonnade designed as a Peripatos walk for strolling while studying; acres of stacks; lecture halls and meeting rooms that seated thousands; reading rooms; acquisition and cataloging departments; warehouses for shipping and receiving; a domed dining hall with an observation tower; banquet areas; gardens; and a zoo stocked with exotic animals from the far-flung empire.

Carved into walls above the shelves: "The place of the cure of the soul."

Burning questions

We have no defining incident about the library's destruction, other than that fire devoured the complex. Perhaps there was one catastrophic blaze, more likely others – one huge disaster would surely have yielded detailed record. Several theories persist, none with historic certainty – but where there's smoke there may be fire:

The name of Julius Caesar, oddly enough, appears down the centuries as possible arsonist-in-chief. In 48 BCE we know that Caesar set fire to one hundred one Egyptian ships at Alexandria and that the fire spread to the docks. Some sources maintained that the blaze got out of control and spread to the Great Library, although that seems improbable since the site was at a distance removed from the harbor.

Theophilus the Patriarch remains a likely Christian suspect for many historians. As an early Church father, he struggled with pagans for command of the city. We know that in 391 CE the fanatical Theophilus destroyed the Serapeum library, converted the temple into a church and "had the phalli of Priapus carried through the midst of the Forum…and the heathen temples were therefore razed to the ground." The Mousseon and the Great Library may have fallen victim in the same campaign. For some sources, end of story.

For others it continues with Cyril, the nephew of Theophilus and successor as patriarch. Riots broke out when a Christian monk was publicly killed by the city prefect under the influence of Hypatia. The last head librarian, she was a brilliant mathematician and philosopher. One day in March 415, during Lent, her chariot was seized by a Christian mob, possibly monks. In a famous death scenario, Hypatia was stripped, dragged naked through the streets, and suffered torture and a brutal murder. For some sources, the death of Hypatia effectively also marked the end of the library.

For others, the round-up of historical suspects continued much later and included a Muslim, Caliph Omar, who occupied the city in 640. When a general asked him what to do about the library holdings, the Caliph reputedly said, "They will either contradict the Koran, in which case they are heresy, or they will agree with it so they are superfluous." As a result, allegedly the texts were used as sauna tinder for the conquerors, taking a suspiciously fanciful six months to burn the collection.

Stirring historical ashes

The legends of destruction are disparate in time and appearances. Some offer intriguing religious or political backstories. Only Plutarch, for instance, faulted Julius Caesar for destruction of the library. While Caesar's memoirs contain a report of burning the harbor as wartime strategy, nowhere does the hero mention the library aflame. But diarists tend to have selective memories, and Caesar was not inclined to record unflattering events for posterity.

As for the Christian connection, *The Decline and Fall of the Roman Empire* provides the account of Theophilus and his struggle for pagan Alexandria. But Edward Gibbon, an eighteenth-century English historian, was called "the noblest Roman" to his delight. A lapsed Catholic, he had "felt the breezes of French rationalism" and was in no way hesitant to blame the Church fathers for converting temples to churches and for the fiery library catastrophe.

Denunciation of the Caliph Omar of Damascus was the handiwork of Gregory of Cappadocia, thirteenth-century Bishop of Alexandria. A militant foe of the Muslim faith, his allegation was so biased and appeared so many centuries after the fact that historians consider his account unlikely. Nor does the report of using the library texts for six months of "bathhouse tinder" add credence.

So many "truthies," as satirist Stephen Colbert calls them, so little direct evidence. But beyond the uncertainty about the library's demise, what we mourn deeper down is the loss of the ancient world's unique source of knowledge, our superb human heritage.

– BARBARA STACY

Postscript: *A modern Bibliotheca Alexandrina arose in 2003, partly sponsored by UNESCO and an effort to reflect ancient glory. Shaped like a disc, the architecture symbolizes the sun of Egypt illuminating the world. It is fireproof.*

Meditation
for the
Demotivated

IT IS WRITTEN that there are many paths leading to Enlightenment. Some are more well-traveled than others. I've been down a lot of them in my lifetime. It would be an understatement to say that some paths are longer than others or that not all of them are lit by neon or even have rest stops along the way. Yet, as any seasoned traveler knows, it's always best to focus on the road that lies ahead, rather than worry about the miles of pavement left behind.

While working as a freelance writer in New York City in the 1980s, I was asked to write a magazine article about a self-styled, contemporary magician. It seemed incredible to me that a young man residing in the middle of a major metropolis could live the life of a medieval sorcerer. He allegedly used magic in the most incredible ways, including calling up and commanding ancient spirits to do his bidding and using ancient alchemical rituals to conjure money from thin air. My research into this modern day hocus-pocus aroused in me a deep curiosity to learn more about alternative forms of spirituality.

The meaning of life

I had already tried Christianity, the religion of my parents, but found it too limited a belief system. Beyond the "heaven or hell" finale, there was little there to stir my imagination. It was like a Broadway musical that couldn't dance or sing. My magician friend was making daily withdrawals from his spiritual ATM and, for a while, I was tempted to follow suit. But being the deep thinker that I am, I had to admit that what I wanted – even more than tens and twenties – was to tune into something that was greater than me.

So I wandered around for a few years contemplating the meaning of life. Why are we here? What is my purpose? What or who is "god"? What is "enlightenment" and how can I find it?

The essence of all things

It was about this time that a friend died unexpectedly and bequeathed me a well-read copy of a book called the *Tibetan Book of the Dead*. I'm sure most people would have preferred real estate, but I like books. I read the book several times and found in each reading a deep and profound sense of peace. One of the passages read: *The essence of all things is one and the same, perfectly calm and tranquil, and shows no signs of becoming.*

What I extracted from this simple statement is that the world may seem like a big and scary place, all complex and oh-my-god-how-am-I-going-to-deal-with-this. But, in reality, all the drama boils down to different variations on a single theme, that being the fact that we are all alive in this space and time and – like it or not – we are all in this together.

All are One

At the most basic cellular level, all things are one thing. We are all the same. The differences are illusions. Rich or poor, young or old, we are all bunkmates on the way to Nirvana.

The "calm and tranquil" part of the affirmation seemed important. Life, at times, was anything but. So I decided to try to find my bliss through meditation.

It seemed easy enough. Sit quietly, close my eyes, and go to my happy place. Breathe deeply. Clear my mind of internal noise. Eliminate distractions, block negative thoughts. Eventually the material world and its delusions will fade away and my true inner light will shine. All of these efforts came to a screaming halt at the point when I tried to quiet my mind.

Quieting internal chat lines

First of all, a lot of crap goes on in there. I'm always thinking. Usually my thoughts are more mundane than profound. I'm thinking about work, my "to do" list, and what's for dinner. I'm worrying about money or whether or not the car will need repairs that I can't afford. I think about the past a lot, reliving entire conversations in my head. Or I daydream about the future and what I want to be when I have to finally grow up. It's hard to shut down the internal chat lines.

I also have a short attention span and find it difficult to sit still for long periods of time. I fidget a lot, shifting my weight from one side to the other, crossing and uncrossing my legs every few minutes. And why is it that, whenever I try to be perfectly calm and tranquil, some unreachable part of my body starts to itch?

Some of the books on meditation suggest chanting a mantra. "Om Mani Padme Hum" is quite popular, as is the shorter version, "Om." I find that these methods work for a brief period of time, but then my mind starts trying to find a way around them. Mundane thoughts return, weaving themselves in and around the mantra, in a way that makes them less obvious, for example, "Om… Om… Om… Too Tired To Be Doing This."

The inner well

However, perseverance and good humor eventually paid off. I was able, after many years of failing miserably, to develop my own brand of meditation. I sit comfortably, which is typically in a comfy chair and not the lotus position. I relax as best as I can, without obsessing about the fact that I'm still conscious of the world around me. If my nose itches, I scratch it. When mundane thoughts trot through the landscape of my mind, I let them graze freely. It is more distracting to move the elephant out of the kitchen, than to politely acknowledge that it's there and walk around it.

I visualize a pool of water – a well of sorts – in my belly. The surface of the water is usually moving, sometimes gently rippling and at other times splashing around like a jug of water being carried on the back of a mountain goat.

My goal is simply to calm the water until it is perfectly still. I know that I've succeeded when I see the reflection of my face in the pool of water. I sustain this mental image for as long as possible, typically just a few minutes. But a lot can happen in those few moments of bliss.

Becoming

That, of course, leaves us with the last part of the affirmation: "and shows no signs of becoming," as if "becoming" is a bad thing. Perhaps another passage from the *Tibetan Book of the Dead* might help us to understand this great mystery:

Whatever is here, that is there and what is there, the same is here.

Huh?

– JIMAHL DI FIOSA

VENUS CLAY FIGURES

Earth's ancient sacred mothers

VENUS figurines are small clay sculptures of women, portrayed with exaggerated features that strongly suggest the late stages of pregnancy. These intriguing art pieces have been found scattered in Stone Age settlements at excavation sites throughout Europe and Asia, especially in France, Russia and Germany.

Created between 33,000 – 9,000 BCE, these female statuettes are actually made of many different materials. Some Venus figurines are fashioned of soft stone, such as calcite and limestone, while others are crafted from bone, ivory and wood. The clay figurines, however, are thought to be the oldest. Averaging about 4 inches long, they were designed to be portable.

By modern standards, these figurines, with their huge stomachs, pendulous breasts, wide hips and hefty legs, would be described as pudgy, even obese. However, in the long ago mists of time, their fatness was venerated, rather than criticized. Perhaps, amid the bleak remnants of the last Ice Age, in the harsh prehistoric, Paleolithic climate, so much colder than today, they projected a strong, prosperous, healthy image.

The Venus of Dolni Vestonice

On July 13, 1925, a clay figurine of a woman with a child's fingerprint embedded in it was discovered at a Paleolithic archeological site in what is now Moravia, in the Czech Republic. This statuette, dubbed the Venus of Dolni Vestonice, is thought to be the world's oldest example of ceramic art. Although scholars consider it unlikely that the art work was made by one so young, the finger print, left in the wet clay about 31, 000 years ago, sparked speculation that the many ancient and mysterious clay images of women were actually prehistoric toys. Other theories suggest that they are objects of goddess worship, good luck emblems or self-portraits of expectant mothers. Alternatively they may have been used for healing or as educational tools. They may even have served as primitive pornography.

Archeologists use the term "Venus Figurines" as something of an umbrella term to conveniently categorize these clay images, although they predate the goddess for whom they are named, by thousands of years. Venus, the classical patroness of beauty and love, dates only from the 4th century BCE.

Venus pudica

In 1864, Marquis Paul de Vibraye playfully described a corpulent Venus statue discovered at Laugerie-Basse in the Vezere valley and lacking arms or feet, as *Venus pudica* or "immodest Venus." He joked that she made no attempt to hide her nudity. Prior to this, the clay ladies were often called *les poires* or "pears," because of their body types.

The term "Venus clay images" really took hold when Edouard Piette adopted the name Venus for a statue he discovered in 1892. Writings hint that Piette was impressed by the statue's prominent labia, which protrudes from the pubic area. Delicately, he referred to this as her *mont de Venus* or mound of Venus.

Venus of Willendorf

Discovered in 1908 along the Danube River in Austria, the Venus of Willendorf, created about twenty-five thousand years ago, is among the most famous of these earliest surviving images of the human body. Her face is featureless, but her head is exquisitely engraved with seven circles (a significant and magical number) of beautiful horizontal bands, which may be a headdress or rows of braided hair. Her body is skillfully depicted, detailing her navel, knee caps and other anatomical particulars.

Some Venus images appear as two dimensional plaques. The ubiquitous voluptuous mother figure is predominant, but other small Stone Age statuettes of children, men and animals have also been found. We really don't why they were created. Perhaps some of the allure of the Venus clay images lies in the profound mystery that surrounds them.

Age of the Great Mother

Astrology offers some insights. There is a cycle of world ages, each spanning about two thousand years. For example, we are currently leaving the Age of Pisces and entering the Age of Aquarius. The Age of Cancer, at least 10,000 years ago in the cycle of the astrological Great Ages, correlates with the creation of the Venus clay images. The July 13th event chart for the discovery of Venus of Dolni Vestonice marks her rebirth in the modern world. This took place when the Sun was transiting Cancer, the zodiac sign ruled by the moon. Motherhood, matriarchs, family life, home, and food are all associated with Cancer. This supports the hypothesis that the clay goddesses acknowledge a belief in motherhood, honor the cycles of birth and the universal need to be nurtured.

– DIKKI-JO MULLEN

The Wicker Man

THE LEGENDARY and mysterious Wicker Man can be traced back to the wealthy tombs of Egypt's pharaohs, where, during excavations, archeologists discovered wonderful and long-buried items, including chairs, baskets, and treasure chests, woven of reeds, branches, swamp grasses and other indigenous plants.

Wicker has been in use for thousands of years. From Egypt, wicker ware made its way to Italy: containers and furnishings were found amid the ruins of Pompeii. With the expansion of the Roman Empire, the material gradually began to appear throughout Europe. That's where it was dubbed wicker; from the Middle English word *wiker*, derived from a Scandinavian root word *weik*, meaning 'to bend.'

During the Iron Age, from about 1200 BCE – 400 CE, woven wicker patterns influenced Celtic art. During this era, human effigies constructed from wicker began to appear in the

British Isles and in Scandinavia. Julius Caesar noted in his *Commentarii de Bello Gallico* (Commentary on the Gallic War) that the Druid priests of the Pagan Celts created large wicker statues – human effigies – for sacrificial burning.

The geographer Strabo supports Caesar's description of the Wicker Man. Both reported that the wicker effigies resembled cages. Living men were placed inside and then the sticks were set on fire, making a sacrificial tribute to the gods. Usually thieves and other criminals were offered, as they were most pleasing to the deities. However sometimes, if no scoundrels were available, innocent men would be set ablaze.

A benevolent wicker man

Wicker mannequins continued to appear in spiritual ceremonies during the medieval era. The *Commenta Berensia*, a tenth century manuscript, describes how the living were burnt inside wicker effigies. Throughout the centuries, the practice of making a wicker structure for burning continued, although gradually the element of human sacrifice encased within faded. An 18th century illustration depicts a benevolent Wicker Man towering over a field at harvest time, as if guarding the crops and field workers.

The Wicker Man, a 1973 cult horror film directed by Robin Hardy, revived the earlier nightmarish practices. The plot unfolds on a remote and sinister island off the Scottish coast. A visitor investigating a modern Pagan cult on the island is burned alive within a Wicker Man. In 2006, Nicholas Cage starred in the American remake of the film, set on a private island in Puget Sound, off the coast of Washington State.

Revival of the wicker man

Perhaps the films have helped to inspire the current revival of interest in the Wicker Man among Neo-Pagan groups. To the modern witch, the Wicker Man appears in a variety of ways. Sometimes he merges with the Green Man as an idol of protection for the forest, kind of an ecological patron. Often Wicker Man images are very artistic and complex. They might not be burned, but are treasured instead as magical keepsakes.

Today these humanoid figures range from miniature pocket pieces to life-sized images to oversized, massive figures, reminiscent of the Jolly Green Giant. The larger structures, designed for burning, are generally lit as the finale at Pagan events. They tend to be made of flexible branches, such as willow, woven around a heavier wooden frame.

Burning women

In Kirkcudbrightshire, Scotland there is an annual rock concert, an outdoor festival spanning several days, which is dedicated to the Wicker Man. The main event on the last night is the burning of the wooden effigy. Ever since 1986, a similar week-long event, called "The Burning Man," has taken place in Black Rock Desert, Nevada. In England, an effigy called The Willow Man has

fared better. It has been maintained as a permanent tribute to the ancient and mysterious figure of the Wicker Man. In 2000, the musical group Iron Maiden toured with a mechanical special effects version, honoring their song "The Wicker Man."

In Northern Italy, a female wicker effigy called *la Vecchia* or the Old Lady is burned in annual village festivals. Frederico Fellini's film *Amarcord* depicts this custom, which takes place on mid-Lent Thursday. Burning a female effigy also occurs in Denmark at *Sankt Hans Aften*, an annual Saint John's Eve Midsummer celebration. The ladies project a vaguely Christian connotation, while the males remain unabashedly Pagan.

– Marina Bryony

Florida's Turtle Mound

An ancient earth sculpture's enduring magic

THOSE who built it vanished long ago, but the giant turtle remains. Named for its distinctive shape, Turtle Mound, located on State Road A1A, just south of New Smyrna Beach, Florida is the largest shell midden on the United States mainland. Over fifty feet tall and over six-hundred feet long, Turtle Mound covers two acres and is visible from at least seven miles at sea. In pre-historic times, it was even higher: Archaeologists suggest it was once at least seventy-five feet tall.

This ancient archaeological site is located on a narrow tract of land at the Canaveral National Seashore, between the Atlantic Ocean and the Indian River, near such popular tourist destinations as Walt Disney World and Daytona Beach. Visitors who climb Turtle Mound enjoy an unforgettable view – particularly magnificent at sunset. Spiritual seekers, especially those who meditate at the top of Turtle Mound, describe profound healing experiences.

Paranormal investigators report the presence of the spirits of the Timucuan (tee-MOO-quan) Indians. Archeologists have dated Timucuan pottery as far back as 800 CE.

Turtle Mound was apparently constructed by the Timucuan from refuse over a period of seven centuries. It is predominately formed from oyster shells, but the remains of bows and arrows, blow guns, spears, and the bones of animals, such as alligators, bear, and deer have also been uncovered.

Why was Turtle Mound built?

Turtle Mound is located at an important and strategic location on the shore. In 1605, the Spanish explorer and cartographer, Alvaro Mexia noted that the Timucuan launched dug-out canoes from the site. It may have been used as a base for fishing and hunting. Another theory is that Turtle Mound was a refuge, a place of safety on high ground during hurricanes.

The Timucuan lived throughout the northern part of Florida and were once the largest indigenous group in this region. They settled far inland, as well as along the coast. During the 1650s, the Timucuan population diminished drastically. Wars with Europeans, as well as with other, more aggressive, Indian tribes are thought to be the primary cause. A series of epidemics, especially smallpox, also contributed to their decimation. The last surviving Timucuan were apparently assimilated into the Seminole nation.

The Timucuan, a deeply spiritual people, are known to have engaged in ceremonies to honor the dead, as well as to bless the harvest and the hunt. They brewed a black tea made from yaupon holly, a potent stimulant, used to induce visions. Archeological evidence and historical records indicate that the Timucuan engaged in farming corn, squash, pumpkins, and melons. Women prepared animal hides and wove fabrics for clothing. The Timucuan constructed elaborate and permanent villages. They built two types of houses. One, a round structure, was covered in palm leaves.

The other was a long house with a bark-covered frame. Meals were apparently taken in communal areas.

Turtle Mound was added to the U.S. National Register of Historic Places on September 29, 1970 and is managed by the National Park Service. A series of historic plaques offer visitors more information. There is a small admission fee.

– ELAINE NEUMEIER

3, 4, 5...

Shamrocks, their genetic variants, and good fortune

May fortune be with you, Wherever you go,
And your blessings outnumber the shamrocks that grow!
TRADITIONAL IRISH TOAST

SHAMROCKS are unmistakably recognizable as the symbol of Ireland, encompassing both Pagan and Christian ideas of trinity: the most common form of the shamrock boasts three emerald green leaves, each balanced delicately opposite the others. Sometimes, however, whether because of genetic variations, environmental factors, or just plain luck, a shamrock may emerge as the legendary four-leaf clover or – with even less frequency – as the tumultuous five-leaf variety. But before we discuss the relative merits of these mutations, let's clarify the word "shamrock."

There is some disagreement as to what constitutes a shamrock. The word derives from the Irish Gaelic word *seamroge*, which means "tiny clover," however plants as diverse as wood sorrel and blackweed are also sometimes known as "shamrocks." The traditional Irish shamrock is the suckling clover, whereas North Americans consider shamrocks to be white clover. For simplicity's sake, this article will define a shamrock as a trefoil plant of petite size.

Shamrock as trinity

A common story maintains that St. Patrick, in an effort to explain the holy trinity to ignorant Druids, turned to the shamrock. Each leaf represented one aspect of a single God: the Father, the Son, and the Holy Ghost. The Druids were said to be so moved by this manifestation of God in nature that Christianity spread as far and wide as the shamrock itself. In reality, the Druids were already quite familiar with the power of trinities and triads and subsequently regarded the shamrock with due respect. The shamrock was also highly valued as a symbol of fertility, as it grew so easily.

FOURtunate finds

For every ten thousand shamrocks that pop up along the countryside, perhaps one will sport a fetching extra leaf. In a field of millions, sheer statistical probability suggests the existence of hundreds of lucky clovers to discover. A determined hunter, armed with patience and a keen eye, will eventually be rewarded with a discovery.

Unfortunately, legend holds that the luckiest clovers are those found through happenstance, rather than sustained effort. The harder one searches, the less valuable the four-leaf clover, at least as a totem. However, a four-leaf clover obtained serendipitously can reputedly bestow incredible gifts to the holder.

Those in possession of four-leaf clovers are protected from most curses and ill health. (This belief may stem from clover's medicinal properties, with red and white varieties brewed as curative teas by many indigenous therapeutic systems.) The bearer of a four-leaf clover can detect previously invisible magic. This includes catching sight of the myriad magical creatures at work all around us. Four-leaf clovers may also herald the arrival of a soul mate.

Too much of a good thing

If four leaves on a clover are good luck, then it stands to reason that five leaves would be even luckier, right? Well, not so fast. A great deal of disagreement exists as to whether or not five-leaf clovers are indeed lucky or downright disastrous instead. Some believe that the first three leaves stand for hope, faith, and love; the fourth, for luck; and the fifth leaf for wealth, particularly of the monetary variety. Therefore, anyone finding a five-leaf clover can expect to receive a large sum of money. However, some maintain the opposite to be true, believing five-leaf

clovers to be incontrovertible portents of financial ruin. Perhaps five-leaf clovers are set in fields by faeries wishing to mark the site of buried treasure; when the thoughtless human removes the charm, the treasure becomes unrecoverable. A vengeful faerie will then make sure the human shares in his ill fortune, taking every opportunity to facilitate the poor human's unfortunate turn of luck. If this indeed is the case, the beset human might try appeasing the wronged faerie with coins, baubles, and trinkets. Alternatively, remain on the safe side and simply leave five-leaf clovers where they stand.

Still counting

Variations in the traditional three-leafed shamrock are not limited to two extra leaves. Eight-leaf clovers are especially prized in large parts of Asia, even more than four-leaf ones. Clovers have even been recorded sporting dozens of extra leaves, a clear case of nature just showing off.

– SHANNON MARKS

The Nutcracker Soldier

His life and times

THAT faithful sentinel, the brightly colored nutcracker soldier who guards the joy of Christmastide, has had a very long march that began centuries before the emergence of the beloved holiday ballet named for him. He is now a theme of winter holiday celebrations world over.

The nutcracker hero's journey began in the thirteenth century in Seiffen, a mining village nestled in the Ore Mountains (Erzgebirge) that now form a border between Germany and the Czech Republic. During the summer months the villagers worked hard in the mines, which were rich in copper, iron and other metals. The heavily wooded mountains above held an even greater treasure: exceptional timber. During the cold winters, the miners were drawn to woodcraft. Over the span of four centuries, as the mines began to be depleted, woodcarving was transformed into a means of livelihood. In the late 1500s lathes, powered by water streaming swiftly down from the mountains, added a whole new dimension to the production of marvelous wooden items.

Among the most popular of these wooden figures were nutcrackers. Originally created as toys for children, they were carved into familiar figures – town criers, miners, chimney sweeps, animals and others. The most popular, however, was always the soldier. Although beautifully crafted, many of these early examples were not yet appreciated as a collector's item. Treated as children's play toys and actually used to crack nuts, they broke easily. Most ended up tossed on the fire. Very few of these original nutcrackers survive today.

Whimsical treasures

By 1745, however, perceptions of these decorative nutcrackers changed. Peddlers at the renowned Dresden Fair marketed a variety of nutcrackers from the Erzebirge region. Nutcrackers became the "must have" purchase – the "Tickle Me Elmo" of their day.

In 1872, Wilhelm Fuchtner (1844-1923), a native of Seiffen, perfected the mass production of nutcrackers. Many different procedures were involved in manufacturing a nutcracker, from turning beech, alder and spruce wood on a lathe to painting the different parts for assembly. Fairy-tale characters and historical figures were designed, but the soldier remained the favorite. Even today, Fuchtner's relatives continue to reside in Seiffen where they create whimsical wooden treasures. Still fashioned from Fuchtner's prototypes, nutcrackers have made his hometown famous and are exported to collectors around the world, especially in the United States.

Nutcracker versus the Mouse King

In Dresden, author E.T.A. Hoffman, found inspiration in the nutcrackers. In 1816, he wrote the story that transformed nutcracker history. His story, *Nutcracker and the Mouse King*, became the basis for Peter Illyich Tchaikovsky's famous ballet *The Nutcracker*, first performed in 1892. The San Francisco Ballet first introduced *The Nutcracker* to American audiences in 1944.

In 2008 the ever popular nutcracker was selected by the United States Postal Service as a holiday stamp design. Four bright and amusing figures were commissioned: a drummer with a red drum and green jacket, a military officer in a yellow coat, a king wearing a ruby crown, and finally, holding a lantern and a snowflake-topped staff, Santa Claus.

Many varieties of nutcrackers exist. For more information, please visit the Leavenworth Nutcracker Museum (www.nutcrackermuseum.com).

– ESTHER ELAYNE

Black Cat
Appreciation Day

LET US PAY tribute to black cats. What more appropriate place is there to do so than in the pages of a publication named *The Witches' Almanac*? After all, no animal is more closely associated with witches than the black cat. Although witches certainly also favor cats of other colors and familiars absolutely do derive from many other species – ferrets, rabbits, dogs, and crows, just to name a few – it is the black cat who stars in vintage Halloween paraphernalia and whose very presence in arts and entertainments is often intended as a tell-tale sign of witchcraft.

The association of witches and black cats dates back thousands of years, although, back then, the cats in question were typically bigger. Black leopards, also known as panthers, are the sacred animal of the great Eurasian goddess Kybele, who, according to some legends, was herself a witch, prior to her ascendance to the divine. Black panthers are also the animals most associated with the Maenads, the ecstatic female worshippers of Dionysus. Many scholars perceive the Maenads, also known as Bacchantes, as the precursors of what would eventually evolve into traditional European witchcraft.

Of course, these associations are not limited to Europe: black jaguars (also known as panthers) are the sacred creature of Tezcatlipoca, the Aztec sorcerer supreme, god of magic and transformation. Nor are associations limited to big cats like jaguars and leopards. According to Jewish folk tradition, Lilith, the Queen of Witches and the true first woman whose existence precedes Eve, is able to transform into a black cat. Throughout North Africa, folk belief suggests that djinn can transform into black cats when they wish to travel incognito. It was and is considered extremely bad luck to harm these cats or molest them in any way,

whether intentionally or accidentally, as the djinn's relatives were sure to know and reciprocate.

Hard times for our feline friends

Unfortunately, no such injunction against harming cats existed in Europe and they were persecuted alongside people accused of witchcraft, both during the Burning Times and after. Although all cats fell under suspicion, black cats were especially identified with witches and thus especially persecuted. These suspicions linger, although exceptions exist: in England, for instance, black cats are traditionally considered good luck, while in Scotland, the arrival of a strange black cat upon your doorstep signals impending prosperity – but only if the cat is welcomed and well-treated.

However, in the United States and elsewhere, black cats continue to suffer. There are still many who will cross the street rather than let a black cat cross their paths. Because of superstitions that black cats are unlucky or precisely because of their identification with witchcraft, they are often the last to be adopted from shelters. On average, black cats stay in shelters many months longer than cats of any other color. By extension, a high percentage of euthanized shelter cats are black. (Black dogs, also associated with witches, suffer similar sad circumstances.)

Celebrating Black Cat Appreciation Day

In order to combat these superstitions and protect black cats, a new holiday was established in 2011: August 17th is Black Cat Appreciation Day. The brainchild of Wayne Morris, who sought to honor the memory of his late sister, who loved black cats, the date was chosen to commemorate the anniversary of her death at age thirty-three, just two months after the death of Sinbad, her own beloved black cat.

Social networking sites spread the word and added to the success of the event. In conjunction with Morris' Facebook page, For the Love of Black Cats (Black Cat Appreciation Page), the goals of Black Cat Appreciation Day include dispelling negative superstitions about black cats and encouraging awareness of the joys of living with a black cat. Many shelters now arrange special black cat adoption events to coincide with this new holiday.

– JUDIKA ILLES

Illustration by Elizabeth Pepper

Merry Meetings

A candle in the window, a fire on the hearth, a discourse over tea…

DURING THE EARLY YEARS of the 20th century Pagan Renaissance an enigmatic and colorful character named Gwen Thompson was publicly engaged at a high level with the resurgence of witchcraft in the United States. She was a prolific correspondent with just about every public figure in the fledgling Pagan movement and a frequent contributor to *The Green Egg* – a publication that was arguably the lifeline which bound the movement together during that early era. Gwen ran a small Coven out of her North Haven, CT home from which she mentored initiates in the lore she had inherited from her family line. At the time only a few others identified their Craft heritage as "Traditional Witchcraft."

Not one to pull punches or be shy about her opinions, Gwen called it like she saw and experienced it. Gwen Thompson passed to the Summerland in 1986 and the few published items available to the public are a handful of articles she submitted to *The Green Egg*. This "Virtual Interview" is a collection of excerpts from those articles. Please keep in mind that the original material was published over 30 years ago for a small and select audience.

Many of the Craft organizations operating in the open (circa mid 1970's) are more theologically oriented than magical. Your Tradition has an extensive magical training program based upon both the Folk Magic practices of the British Isles and the Western Magical systems. Can you speak to the requirement for the witch when approaching the Magic Arts?

The ingredients necessary for a successful magical operation are: interest, concentration of will, and emotion. If the operator lacks confidence, the forces involved will not rally to produce the desired results. A successful, positive attitude must inevitably produce positive results. The old saying nothing succeeds like success holds true in all cases. The simple scientific fact that like attracts like cannot be ignored.

Self-doubt is a crippling state of mind that must be overcome before any degree of positive achievement can be reached. Self-doubters generally extend their mental inadequacies over such a wide area that they function in a perpetual atmosphere of impending failure. Their attitudes reach out to others and nobody takes them seriously. The other extreme applies to those who are so involved with what they imagine to be personal power that they strut about like the barnyard rooster doing a great deal of crowing and flapping, until they, too, manage to achieve a similar response. Nobody takes them seriously.

The ideal attitude is one in which the magical practitioner adopts a serious, confident and emotionally determined attitude regarding the working of the rituals. Magic is a very private, personal thing. A degree of humility and respect towards those forces involved is a necessary ingredient. The failure of any magical working generally lies within the functional ability of the practitioner rather than with the ritual. One can train a chimpanzee to ride a bicycle, but it doesn't mean he's going anywhere with it.

Some believe that the Craft is only about doing positive-based, Deosil workings and that cursing has no place in modern witchcraft. What is your take on this aspect of the Craft and magic practice?

There is no getting away from the fact that thoughts and attitudes can and do cause harm when negatively directed. Hate can kill, but the one harboring it pays the greater price. When it is felt that measures must be taken to ensure the protection of oneself or a group, the safest and quite often the surest method is the magical operation involving self-defense. Self defense rituals have a tendency to reverse hostile vibrations and to erect a psychological barrier of protection. The efficacy of such magic comes from repetitive sound and motion which tends to play upon the emotions of the practitioner. The emotions act as the cohesive force for the ritual.

The following is a simple defensive ritual that we have found most effective.

It may be done by an individual or a group. It is not necessary that it be done within a consecrated circle, although this is quite often the case. You will require blue or white candles for each person taking part in the ritual.

All face North and say: "O Guardian of the North Wind, protect us against all evil that may come from the North. Return the evil to its source in the name of Our Lady Diana!"

All face West and say: "O Guardian of the West Wind, protect us against all evil that may come from the West. Return the evil to its source in the name of Our Lady Diana!"

All face South and say: "O Guardian of the South Wind, protect us against all evil that may come from the South.

Circa early 1970s

October 1981

Return the evil to its source in the name of Our Lady Diana!"

Then all face East and say: "O Guardian of the East Wind, protect us against all evil that may come from the East. Return the evil to its source in the name of Our Lady Diana!"

Light the blue or white candles which you must carry as you walk widdershins (anti-clockwise) chanting:

> *To bane, to bane...*
> *Begane, begane.*
> *Thrice take ye doun*
> *From whence ye came!*

This chant must be continued for 15 minutes. At the end of that time, stop abruptly and making your mind as blank as possible, stare fixedly at the lower part of the candle flame (the blue section) for a minute or so. Then extinguish the candles. The candles used for this ritual must be discarded preferably in a brown paper bag containing flour.

You say that the Craft you practice and teach is Traditional; passed down from generation to generation in your family. Can you tell us something about what it was like to grow up in a family that practiced witchcraft?

There is only one form of wisdom that time alone can bestow, and that is the lessons learned from experience. Our children were taught to respect the old ones, even though they were often people of little formal education and very simple in their ways. They had lived long and had, therefore, experienced much of life and its ways. Their advice through their own lessons learned was considered invaluable, and thus they were held in deep respect for those things in which they had learned wisdom.

Children were not taught to strive for perfection, but for wisdom. Perfection is a broad concept with different meanings for different people. It actually does not exist. The caution was: "Do not seek perfection in others unless you can give it." Therefore...we have the counsel to "live an let live."

It seems that all witches embrace Halloween with especial enthusiasm. What can you tell us about Halloween in your Tradition?

Who or what is Old Jack? Old Jack is another name for our Great Horned God of the Witches when he appears at the death of the year (Hallows) and takes complete charge over the winter months. As God of Death and Rebirth he reigns over the Hallows festival as Old Jack, and often an effigy is made to represent him. The effigy takes the form of the well known farmer's Scarecrow (and possibly this is where the old farm folk originally got their inspiration for the Scarecrow).

A Covenstead need not be located in a rural area for the members of its coven to construct Old Jack. He can be made as any scarecrow is, and placed in any part of an apartment, house or Circle Room. He can be as easily stuffed with old newspapers or dried leaves, and it is a fun project. Making an effigy of Old Jack is sheer Pagan sport.

May I say to the purists who may chance to read this in no way is such an adventure insulting to our God. Being a God of death and rebirth does not diminish the fact that he is also a God of great joy, mirth and laughter. He may be fierce, he may strike panic wherever he appears, but he also enjoys being acknowledged in happy ways.

For us, All Hallows is not a somber time at all. It is a time to remember our ancestors and commemorate our beloved dead; a time to communicate with them and to let them know we are aware of their existence. It is a time to search into past lives and to gain knowledge from them. To learn from that which has gone before the ideals we believe in.

Let Old Jack guard well your Hallows Circle and impart to him the magicks that you wish. He will not fail you, and soon he will be drawing snow and ice-designs upon some window panes in his aspect as Jack Frost as he rides the Mighty Northwinds.

Circa early 1930s

Spinning the Wheel

A "down under" glance at the witches' year

Pagans and the southern hemisphere

The Wheel of the Year has become the popular emblem for the seasonal cycle of the eight festivals or sabbats celebrated by those who follow the Old Ways. This eternal progression of the seasons is nature's echo of the beginnings, growth, endings, and renewal within the human experience. The Wheel developed from the Pagan traditions of the Northern Hemisphere. Witches living south of the equator in Australia, New Zealand, South Africa, and South America must reverse the Wheel in order to properly honor the agricultural festivals and celebrate the solstices and equinoxes. This guide provides an easy reference for adapting the eight sacred days (Halloween, winter solstice, Candlemas, spring equinox, Beltane, summer solstice, Lammas, and the autumnal equinox) to the seasonal cycles of the Southern Hemisphere. It will enable Wiccans who live or are visiting south of the equator to fully embrace the Craft cycles.

The witches' year of sacred days in the southern hemisphere

Samhain, Halloween: April 30–May 1
It's the Celtic New Year. The intense summer heat has given way to autumn's chill. It's a time to reflect, to honor the ancestors. Darkness increases quickly. The veil between this world and the next grows thinner. Other dimensions open. Death is welcomed and embraced as a part of rebirth. The Crone brings her wisdom and experience.

Yuletide, Winter Solstice: June 21–23
This is the longest night and the shortest of days. The Yule log is lit. Witches may gather to keep a vigil all night, preparing to welcome the sunrise. The promise of a new season of growth and productivity out of the darkness and cold is anticipated. The God is reborn from the Goddess. She withdraws to take her rest.

Imbolc, Candlemas: August 1
Imbolc is about the coming of spring and the birth of animals. New growth welcomes the increasing sunlight. The Earth awakens and starts to stir.

Ostara, Spring Equinox: Sept. 21–23
Now it is the halfway point between winter and summer when the days and nights are nearly equal in length. Light replaces the darkness. It's a time of discovery, innocent curiosity, and youthful exuberance. Flowers, sprouts, and eggs are part of the imagery.

Beltane, Novey Eve: October 31
Summer's peak time begins with fertility festivals, handfastings, and

sporting events. Bright colors and joy prevail. The passionate union of God and Goddess is celebrated. This day is called Novey Eve (November Eve) in Australia.

Midsummer's Day, Summer Solstice: December 21–23
The longest day of the year arrives. This fire festival marks a peak of joy and strength. Nature's power is at its brightest and best. The God appears at his most powerful, while the fruitful Goddess watches over the abundant Earth.

Lammas, Lughnassad: February 2
Loafmass is sacred to the loaves of harvest grains and other crops. The Sun King is descending, offering his life force to the land. The Goddess completes her role as mother and begins to become the crone. It's time to reflect upon the year's successes. Change is welcomed as an essential part of growth.

Mabon, Autumnal Equinox: March 21–22
Day and night are nearly equal again. A thanksgiving for the final harvest of the year is offered, and autumn fruits are gathered. Food stores are prepared; home and heritage are appreciated. Commitments to family and the Craft of the Wise are renewed. Cool breezes hint at the winter ahead and illustrate how the Goddess mourns the God, yet keeps him with her to eventually be reborn at Yule.

–Dikki-Jo Mullen

Tsukimi
The harvest moon

EVER SO QUIETLY, in the eighth month of the lunisolar calendar, on the eve of the full moon, all across Japan, families and friends gather to admire the bright mid-autumn harvest moon and eat moon cakes. According to ancient lore, this moon is the fullest and brightest, due to the positions of the earth, sun and moon. The confluence of their relative positions makes it the ideal time for viewing and honoring.

Tsukimi – literally "moon-viewing"– is the magical festival that honors the autumnal moon, as well as the summer harvest that has just concluded and the rice harvest that is about to begin. The evening begins at the family altar, with offerings made to the moon. Pampas grass is arranged in a vase and placed prominently, together with offerings of white rice dumplings (*Tsukimi dango*), taro, edamame, chestnuts, and sake. These foods are so profoundly connected with Tsukimi that alternative names for the festival include *Imomeigetsu* (Potato Harvest Moon), *Mamemeigetsu* (Bean Harvest Moon), and *Kurimeigetsu* (Chestnut Harvest Moon). Each of these foods transmits its own blessing. For example, dumplings are said to bring happiness and good health. These offerings are piled high, as a reflection of the moon's beauty and to serve as a reminder of the deep gratitude for the autumn harvest. The family, kneeling with their offering, gives collective thanks for the bountiful summer harvest, while offering further prayers toward a good rice harvest to come.

Let the festivities begin!

With the obligations of prayers and offerings finished at the home shrine, the festivities move outdoors. Gathering in a spot where the full moon can be clearly seen, family and friends enjoy an evening of storytelling and poetry recitation, while basking in the silver rays of the moon. Families will often gather by a lake or stream, so that the light and beauty of the full moon can be appreciated, not only in the sky, but also as reflected beauty. A blanket is laid on the ground, as if for a picnic. Again offerings are laid out, so that the moon itself can partake of these humble gifts. Silver cups ward off any evil spirits seeking to trouble the gathering.

Among the stories that may be repeated is one that has been told across the region since time immemorial. This is a simple Buddhist story of humility and selflessness told through the eyes of a hungry old man and his animal companions:

There once was a very old and very hungry old man, who asked his companions the monkey, the otter, the jackal, and the rabbit for food. The monkey immediately collected fruits and gave them freely to the old man. The otter went bouncing through the waters and brought him a fish. The jackal spied a lizard and brought it to the old man. Alas, the poor little rabbit had nothing to bring. He knew the grasses that he ate would not give the poor old man sustenance. In a moment of selflessness, the rabbit decided he could only offer his own body and so he jumped into the fire to cook himself. Surprisingly, the selfless rabbit's body would not burn, because, in fact, the man was neither old nor hungry, he was an enlightened one teaching selflessness. Because the rabbit was so selfless, the old man drew rabbit's image in the moon to remind all of rabbit's act.

At the end of this story, many parents will gather their children, pointing to the outlines of the rabbit in moon, who, using his wooden hammer, pounds the rice to make delectable rice dumplings. Children take delight at every month's full moon, but most especially at Tsukimi.

Another story that might be told is the story of the bamboo cutter, his wife, and the moon princess:

There once lived an elderly man who made his living by cutting bamboo. One day, as was usual, he went to gather bamboo in the fields and hills not far from his home. While in the fields this day, he found a very unique piece of bamboo. So unique was this piece of bamboo that, when he cut it, a very beautiful little girl appeared. He took this lovely little girl as his daughter and he and his wife looked after her well. The wondrous little girl grew up to be a beautiful woman, who, at the proper age, was

asked by five separate noblemen to be their wife. But she would have none of them, as she was a princess who had come from the moon. Once she had refused of all the suitors, she returned to the moon from whence she came and to this day looks down at us with her magical face.

Predictions and challenges

The Japanese, in the days of yore, were aware of the moon and the cycles through which it passes. The old calendars closely aligned the days, the month, and the seasons with the moon. Each day was aligned to a specific moon phase. The new moon would always fall on the first of the month and the full on the fourteenth. Each day in-between was marked against the face of the moon. Thus, it was possible, on many specific dates, to predict the shape that the moon would take on that particular night.

While in these times, as many live in urban settings, it can be challenging to enjoy a traditional outdoor Tsukimi gathering, many still observe the festival with indoor feasting and storytelling. It is also celebrated at temples and shrines, such as the Shimogamo shrine in Kyoto.

> *Viewing the moon,*
> *no one at the party*
> *has such a beautiful face*
> — Matsuo Basho

— DEMETRIUS SANTIAGO

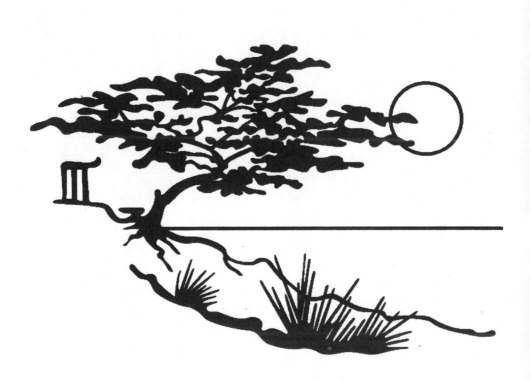

126

～ Tsukimi Treats ～

PERHAPS THIS YEAR, you would like to enjoy Tsukimi with a taste of moon cakes or rice dumplings:

Moon Cakes
Filling Ingredients:
1 can of lotus seed paste
1/4 cup finely chopped walnuts

Dough Ingredients:
4 cups all-purpose flour
1/2 cup non-fat dried milk powder
3 teaspoons baking powder
1/2 teaspoon salt
3 eggs
1 cup sugar
1/2 cup solid shortening,
   melted and cooled
1 egg yolk, lightly beaten

Preparation:
1. Mix lotus seed paste and walnuts together in a bowl and then set aside.
2. Sift flour, milk powder, baking powder, and salt together into a bowl.
3. In a large bowl, beat eggs, and then add sugar and beat for 10 minutes.
4. Add the melted shortening to this mixture and mix lightly.
5. With a spatula, fold in flour mixture.
6. Turn dough out onto a lightly floured board and then knead until smooth.
7. Divide dough in half;
8. Roll each half into a log.
9. Cut each log into 12 equal pieces and roll each piece of dough into a ball.
10. Roll each ball out onto a lightly floured board, making a 3.5-inch circle about one-eighth inch thick.

11. Put a dollop of lotus seed paste mixture into the center of each and then fold it in half, crimping the sides to enclose the filling.
12. Place the cakes on an ungreased baking sheet and brush the tops with egg yolk. Bake in a preheated 375° F oven for 30 minutes or until golden brown. Allow the cakes to cool before eating.

Rice Dumplings
Ingredients:
1 cup of rice flour
1/3 cup warm water
2 tablespoons of sugar
(Optional flavorings may be added to the rice flour, for example, extracts, concentrated flavorings, powdered spices, espresso powder, coconut powder, cocoa, and powdered milk)

Preparation:
1. Lightly mix the flour, sugar and any flavorings that you may wish to use within a large mixing bowl.
2. Slowly add the water to the flour, then knead, until the dough is well combined. (It will not be a smooth dough.)
3. Form 15 small round dumplings.
4. Bring water to a boil in a medium sized pot, gently ladle in the balls.
5. Wait until the majority of the dumplings are floating and then cook for an additional minute.
6. Remove from heat, adding cold water to cool the dumplings. Complete the cooling process on a mesh tray.

Mystical Number Chants

Esoteric numerology

1 2 3 4 5 6 7 8 9 0

VARIOUS magical traditions from all over the world link specific numbers with success, healing, and power. "The third time is the charm" is the perfect example, reflecting the ancient belief that a prayer or affirmation must be repeated three times to be put into motion.

Some years ago, W. F. "Doc" Wyatt, the well-known spiritual investigator and world traveler from Brevard County, Florida, met a high priestess in Venezuela. During a ceremony held deep in the jungle, she channeled a series of number blessings from her spirit guides. Although it may be impossible to determine why they work, chanting the various number combinations she received that night has proved beneficial for many. To maximize their power, use these number invocations often. They are extremely effective and easy. Give it a try.

For example, to spiritually purify and bless food, just say "9- 9- 5" over the plate. When groups of aspiring ghost hunters gather, it is a good idea for them to memorize the numbers which set up a shield of strong protection by saying "nine times nine" aloud. (Not "nine times nine equals eighty-one" or "nine, nine, nine" – just "nine times nine.") Your own intuition may suggest other personal number combinations to experiment with, however the following are those received by Doc Wyatt:

9 x 9   provides a powerful protective shield, especially beneficial against unfriendly ghosts

3 x 1   closes portals to other dimensions or to the Other Side

5 x 7   shields your home or car against robbery

5 x 8   sends love to a place or person – try this one to bless the USA.

3 x 5   removes hidden souls

8 x 2   enhances personal charisma

5 x 1   attracts money and abundance

7 x 4   closes portals to other planets

3 x 0   helps connect to your higher self

7 x 1   protects your inner senses

5 x 2   raises the energy level, physically, mentally, and emotionally

1 x 0   provides greater physical energy

3 x 3   provides harmony and activity in the chakras

9 x 3   magnifies creativity

2 x 1   clears out old programming

7 x 0   calms, clears fears, restores control

17 x 3 enhances neutrality and objectivity

14 x 1 attracts attention – try this to get a love interest to take notice!

3 x 12 generates perfect ideas and raises the kundalini

10 x 1 provides greater attunement of the higher senses and psychic ability

7 x 5   invokes harmony regarding material responsibilities, such as car and house payments

10 x 2 attracts prosperity

13 x 1 clears the cosmos of discordant energies

12 x 8 shields against separation or rejection

8 x 0   clears Elementals

14 x 2 clears interference at the Godhead and higher spiritual planes

11 x 2 enhances healing by the laying-on of hands

8-8-8 encourages communication with the Ascended Masters, Great Spirit Council, and other secret elders

Number squares

Magic squares provide yet another way to tap into the esoteric power of numbers. The numbers in these diagrams are arranged so that, when added together, the same sum results, regardless of direction. Magic number squares have fascinated mathematicians and magicians alike since the earliest times. These squares are linked to planets and can contain only nine numbers or more than eighty.

The Square of Saturn is both the simplest and among the most powerful. The sum of each line is 15, no matter which way it's added. The Square of Saturn reputedly protects against enemies, ill health, and the vicissitudes of old age. Make a copy and carry it with you or place it in your home or work place.

– ELAINE NEUMEIER

4	9	2
3	5	7
8	1	6

Om Mani Padme Hum

The jewel in the lotus

SOMETIMES a sound is more than just a sound. The word "mantra" derives from a Sanskrit phrase meaning "that which saves from destruction." A mantra is a sound, word, or a group of words believed to possess powers of transformation. The earliest surviving documentation of mantras is found in the Vedas, the primary sacred texts of Hinduism, but the concept is not limited to Hinduism, but shared by multiple spiritual traditions, including Sikhism, Jainism, and Buddhism. Many mantras exist. Although all may be powerful, not all possess the same powers of transformation. Some mantras are also specifically associated with certain deities, Buddhas, bodhisattvas, and saints.

The most revered of all Buddhist mantras consists of six Sanskrit syllables that have been transliterated into English as Om Mani Padme Hum. (However, pronunciation of this mantra varies, depending on region. For example, the traditional Tibetan pronunciation is Om Mani Peme Hung.) According to the Karandavyuha Sutra, the Buddha himself described it as the most powerful and beneficial of all mantras. It remains the most popular and beloved of Tibetan prayers.

Avalokiteshvara, Kwan Yin, Chenrezig, and the Dalai Lama

This particular mantra is closely associated with the bodhisattva, Avalokiteshvara and his Chinese alter ego, Kwan Yin. Avalokiteshvara is the bodhisattva of compassion, considered to be the special protector of the Tibetan people. It is traditionally believed that chanting, Om Mani Padme Hum, whether silently or aloud, attracts his attention and invokes his blessings, as well as that of Kwan Yin. (Some believe Kwan Yin to merely be the Chinese translation of the name, Avalokiteshvara, just as he is called Chenrezig in Tibetan. Thus they are multiple names for the same sacred being. Others, however,

130

perceive Kwan Yin, the Goddess of Mercy, to be a distinct sacred being.) As the Dalai Lama is considered to be an avatar of Avalokiteshvara, this mantra is closely identified with him and with all Dalai Lamas, past and future.

Om Mani Padme Hum is an extremely popular prayer, so popular that it is often chanted by those who do not comprehend the meaning of the syllables. Nor is comprehension necessary to reap the benefits – the combined sounds themselves are a font of power. Although the mantra's individual components may be translated, this mantra transcends literal translation.

Behold! The Jewel in the Lotus

Typically, Om Mani Padme Hum is translated as "Behold! The jewel in the lotus" or alternatively, "Praise to the jewel in the lotus." There are scholars, who argue, however, that the first and last syllables lack literal translation – they cannot be translated literally – and so, according to them, this mantra may actually mean, "Om Jewel in the Lotus Hum."

Om, the mantra's first syllable, is a mantra in itself. Om is traditionally considered to be the sound of the universe – the primordial vibration that is the root and source of all mantras. The two words in the center can definitely be translated literally. *Mani* means "jewel" or possibly "bead." (Bringing the concept full circle, the English word "bead" derives from a root word indicating prayer. Many spiritual traditions, including Buddhism, feature rosaries or other prayer beads intended to facilitate prayer and chanting.) *Padme* means "lotus" – the sacred flower of Buddhism. Some scholars consider manipadme to be one compound word, literally "jewel-lotus" – possibly an epithet for Avalokiteshvara or yet another of his alternative names.

Six virtues, six realms

Om Mani Padme Hum transcends its literal meaning. Reputedly all the teachings of the Buddha are inherent within this mantra. Each syllable may also be interpreted as representing a Buddhist virtue: generosity, ethics, patience, diligence, renunciation, and wisdom.

It is no random accident that this particular mantra features six syllables. Each syllable possesses the inherent power to purify one of the six Buddhist realms of existence:

- *Om* purifies pride and the realm of the deities
- *Ma* purifies envy, jealousy, the need to be entertained, and the realm of the jealous deities
- *Ni* purifies desire, passion, and the human realm
- *Pad* purifies ignorance, prejudice and the animal realm
- *Me* purifies poverty, acquisitiveness, and the realm of the Hungry Ghosts
- *Hum* purifies hatred, aggression and the Buddhist Hell realms

Chanting Om Mani Padme Hum may thus be understood as a form of self-blessing. Simultaneously, it blesses all living beings and provides for their spiritual liberation, as well as our own. No limitations on chanting this mantra exist: it may be recited thousands of times daily.

Carved and spinning words

Nor is it necessary to chant the words to reap the mantra's benefits. Viewing the written words is believed to possess the same powerful effect. Thus, to increase the mantra's power and efficacy, it is engraved onto jewelry or carved onto rocks for contemplation. Carvings are frequently placed where they can benefit travelers.

Writing the mantra on paper is considered the equivalent of chanting. To further increase the potency, the written mantra may be inserted into prayer wheels – also known as Mani wheels – a traditional Tibetan spiritual technology intended to spread and promote blessings.

In Tibet, wheels were once traditionally reserved for spiritual purposes alone, rather than used for agriculture or transportation, as elsewhere. Rolls of paper imprinted with the Om Mani Padme Hum mantra are wound around the wheel's axle, so that they can be spun virtually endlessly. Small hand-held wheels are most common, but larger wheels also exist. Prayer wheels are also con-structed and situated so that they may be spun by the wind, rising steam, or flowing water.

Many Mani wheels are beautiful. Not only do they contain this sacred mantra, the outside of the wheel may be decorated with its sacred syllables, too. Digital prayer wheels also now exist, as does a phone app. According to His Holiness the Dalai Lama, having the mantra on your computer is equivalent to using a traditional prayer wheel.

– JUDIKA ILLES

Speaking with the Angels

An introduction to the Enochian system of occultism

JOHN DEE (1527-1609) epitomized the Renaissance intellectual. A gifted astronomer who served England's Queen Elizabeth I as her court astrologer – and occasional spy! – Dee was also a prominent mathematician, who wrote a preface to the English edition of Euclid's *Elements of Geometrie*. He developed innovative navigational aids that helped enable the British exploration of the Americas and was a founding fellow of Trinity College, Cambridge. In addition, John Dee was an avid Hermetic magician.

Dee sought to "aspire to an exploration and understanding of the supra-celestial virtues and metaphysical influences." (French, p. 65) In order to do so, he would, in his opinion, have to become like the biblical patriarch Enoch and converse with the holy angels themselves.

Enter Edward Kelley

In 1581, Dee was troubled by unknown knockings in the night, as well as by odd and disturbing dreams. Whatever the reasons for these disturbances, Dee believed that it was time for his magical workings to include a medium able to see, hear, or converse with spirits.

After being unimpressed by the work of Barnabas Saul, a skryer, Dee eventually came into contact with the man who would become the key to unlocking some of the most bizarre mystical workings. His name was Edward Kelley.

Kelley, then approximately 27 years old, had been wandering around England, selling what were reputedly magical elixirs and alchemical concoctions. Formerly an undergraduate at Oxford, Kelley had been summarily dismissed for reasons unknown. Little did either Kelley or Dee know, upon their first meeting, that, for the next seven years, the two of them would be close compatriots and partners in profound occult rituals.

Enter the archangel

During their first recorded skrying session, not only did Dee and Kelley reputedly make contact with the archangel Uriel, but a magical sigil was revealed, along with instructions dictating the construction of a magical pantacle known as the *Sigillum Dei Aemeth*, which was to be used in further sessions. John Dee had found his medium.

Over the following two years, Dee and Kelley regularly performed rituals and séances in order to communicate with Uriel and other spirits that the devout Dee understood to be angels. A series of magical squares were dictated through Kelley, revealing new angelic names and symbols to be employed in the practice of the astrological magic of the Seven Holy Planets. This series of sessions yielded what Dee would deem *De Heptarchia Mystica* or the Heptarchic system of magic.

Forty-nine angels

Also dictated during this period was the construction of various occult instruments, mostly tablets, as well as a system constructed for employing the powers of forty-nine angels (7 X 7) for various tasks. The names of the angels, each constructed out of seven letters, were received through a rather complicated system that involved decoding a cross-shaped table with 343 squares broken up into seven smaller tables, further divided into grids consisting of forty-nine squares each. This was reputedly dictated to the magicians by the archangel Michael during one three-hour session.

Beginning in March 1583, Kelley beheld visions of a book whose leaves needed to be filled. Over the next thirteen months, Dee and Kelley filled them with what would become known as the "angelic language" or *Enochian*, as it is called today.

Twenty-one letters were dictated to the mages, each possessing its own particular name and phonetic value. Over time, an entire language was either created by the magicians or dictated to them from a sacred source, depending upon one's perspective.

According to Dee, the angels told the magicians that this language and the magical system dictated to them had been taught by God to the biblical patriarch Enoch, thousands of years before. Supposedly, God had then purposefully let this wisdom disappear from the world for generations, after "wicked hands" had gained access to it. However, John Dee's fervent prayers and piety had apparently moved the heart of God, so as to once again share this wisdom with humanity.

The Enochian Calls

What are now known as the "calls" of Enochian seem to be the centerpiece of this entire linguistic magical system. These calls are hymns of devotion that are simultaneously invocations to the various holy powers that control and manipulate the universe. The first four of these calls were dictated to Dee and Kelley in a painstaking manner. The angels had voiced fears that the calls were too powerful to be read aloud and therefore had to be read letter by letter in backwards order. Shortly after, the angels gave the translation of the text that had been dictated. Eventually, the angels, not to mention

Dee and Kelley, grew tired of this method: the remaining calls (5-18) were dictated in a more straightforward manner, although the angels would wait six weeks before translating these latter calls.

The East is a house of virgins singing praises amongst the flames of first glory wherein the Lord hath opened his mouth and they are become twenty-eight living dwellings in whom the strength of man rejoiceth, and they are appareled with ornaments of brightness such as work wonders on all creatures. Whose Kingdoms and continuance are as the third and fourth strong towers and places of comfort, the seats of mercy and continuance. O you Servants of Mercy, Move, Appear, sing praises unto the Creator and be mighty amongst us. For to this remembrance is given power and our strength waxeth strong in our Comforter. – English translation of the Seventh Call, as found in Lon Milo DuQuette's book, *Enochian Vision Magick.*

Although the characters of the Enochian language are written from right to left, in the manner of most Semitic languages, its grammar generally follows an English format, containing identifiable pronouns, but lacking any particular verb declension or conjugation. The Enochian language possesses its own grammar and syntax and is not merely glossolalia or a string of names. The word meanings found in each call are entirely consistent with one another, which is remarkable, if we recall that the first four calls were dictated backwards, letter by letter. If the language was indeed created by Dee or Kelley and not dictated by angels, this would be a remarkable feat of mental gymnastics for even the most disciplined minds.

The final key

Eventually, however, mounting tensions between Dee and Kelley reached a fever pitch. Reputedly at the behest of angels, the pair together with their families had been wandering through Europe, settling for a time in Krakow. While Kelley became increasingly distrustful of the angels, Dee still wished to maintain regular contact with them. For this he needed Kelley and so Dee was sometimes forced to resort to bribes or threats. Their magical séances were sometimes disturbed by what Dee and Kelley deemed evil spirits, who attempted to coerce the two into abandoning their project. Even the angels eventually told the two mages that the séance sessions must be completed by August.

The final key to the Enochian magical system – the reception of the names of the thirty *Aethyrs* – occurred on Dee's fifty-seventh birthday, July 13th, 1584. Shortly afterwards, the angels fell silent and, as far as we know, Dee and Kelley were not to communicate with them again.

Dee and Kelley drifted apart. Dee returned to England, while Kelley continued to wander the Continent, pursuing an alchemical career, until his death in 1597 in what is now the Czech Republic.

– ANTHONY TETH

Yoruba Creation Myth

IN A TIME out of mind, there only existed the sky and the great waters below. In the sky lived Olodumare, Creator of all that is and ever shall be; Olodumare, who is neither male nor female, but all. With Olodumare dwelled the primal Orisa, those forces that emanated from Olodumare's very being. Alone, in the great waters below, lived another emanation of Olodumare – Olokun, herself a great Orisa.

As time passed, Olodumare's eldest son, Obatala grew restless and wished to travel beyond sky, but where would he go? There were only two domains in which to exist: the land of the sky and the land of no land, the great waters. In his consternation, he approached Olodumare and asked for permission to venture out of the sky.

Olodumare nodded in consent. However, where would Obatala go? There was nowhere outside of the sky for him to set his feet. The domain of Olokun would not do, for surely he would sink. The space between would not do either, since he would forever float in the infinite void.

Orunmila and the sacred palm nuts

Lacking an answer, Obatala sought the advice of his brother, Orunmila, who is the Orisa who knows all that is, all that was, and all that will be. Obatala sat on the mat of divination as Orunmila brought out the sacred oracle, the voice of destiny itself, the palm nuts known as *Ikin*.

As Orunmila rolled the sacred Ikin in the sacred dust on the divining board before them, he asked Obatala why he was there and what advice he sought. Obatala advised that Olodumare had given consent, but – as only Orunmila could know the voice of Olodumare – he wished to know how this journey could be accomplished.

Esu and Odu

Orunmila prayed intensely to Esu, the only one able to open and close the ways, even over Olodumare's objections. He then entreated each of their brother and sister Orisa. Finally, he marked the first sixteen emanations of Olodumare – the primary Odu that made creation itself. He then pounded the sacred Ikin in his hands to produce the sign that would reveal the voice of Olodumare.

Orunmila began to sing the sacred verses of the Odu, revealing the divine

plan to Obatala and the way his task could be accomplished. Orunmila told Obatala that first he must make sacrifice. He must make offering to Esu. He must offer to the sky and he must offer to the sea. He advised him to come back to perform *ebo* (sacrifice) bringing with him a golden chain, sand, and a five-toed black hen, along with many other items, as well as a goodly amount of cowries for payment.

Ogun, the golden chain and the five-toed hen

Obatala left Orunmila's home to gather the items of ebo. First, he went to all of the Orisa to collect gold, which he then brought to the home of Ogun, requesting that he forge the golden chain required for ebo. Obatala then went to his farm to collect a hen. He looked and looked and, finally amongst the many, he found a single black hen. Grabbing the hen, he counted the toes. There were five and thus this hen would fulfill the ebo.

Obatala then went to the base of the celestial palm tree, the very palm from which the sacred Ikin had been collected. There he saw a goodly amount of sand in which the tree grew. Obatala pulled a snail's shell from his bag and collected the sand that would fulfill the ebo.

Finally, he went to his home to collect the cowries which would pay for the ebo. Obatala collected not only the amount requested – he collected every single cowry that he had. He put these into his bag, so that he could pay Orunmila.

The divine plan

Obatala returned to Orunmila's home. The two sat on the mat again and Orunmila sang the sacred Odu of sacrifice and entreated the sky, the waters, and Esu. He made ebo for Obatala. Again, Orunmila pounded the sacred Ikin and was told by Esu that sacrifice was accepted. He was further instructed what advice to give Obatala.

Orunmila advised Obatala to take the gold chain and hang it from the sky down towards the great waters. He should climb down the chain and sprinkle the sand from the shell onto the great waters. When this was done, Obatala was instructed to drop the black hen onto the sand and from there the land of earth would come into being. Lastly, he was instructed to plant the single Ikin into the new earth.

The birth of Ife

Obatala did not fully understand how all of this would come to be, but thanked Orunmila and went off to do as he was told. He went to the sacred palm tree and hung the golden chain down toward the great waters and began to climb down. When he reached the end of the chain, he reached into his bag and pulled out the snail shell containing the sand. He poured the sand out and it floated atop the great waters, thus creating the first land. This land was called Ife.

Obatala loosed the five-toed black hen onto the newly created Ife. The hen scratched and scratched at the sand that was Ife, spreading it about and creating

from the fruit of the sacred palm and ferment it to make a cool drink called Emu. Obatala and Yemoja celebrated their new home and drank fermented palm wine.

Yemoja and Obatala desire children

Yemoja and Obatala were very happy together and lived peacefully. However, as time went by, they wished for more than each other's companionship. They wished to have children. They talked about this and decided that they would fashion their children from the clay of the land of Ife.

Yemoja and Obatala set out to collect clay for creating their children. They traveled to all the river banks of the vast lands. There were many different kinds of clay: some dark, some light, some with this tint of color, some with another. Having collected much clay, they returned home and rested.

vast lands that surrounded the center that was Ife. Finally, Obatala loosed his hands from the chain and fell onto the land of Ife. He planted the sacred Ikin into the newly created earth and right before his eyes a twin of the sacred palm of the sky instantly grew.

Obatala was pleased with these results and decided he would stay in Ife, this new land. Taking some bark from the sacred palm, he crafted the first structure in Ife, intended to house the spirit of Orunmila. From the sacred palm, he took the first sixteen nuts that would be the voice of Olodumare in this new place. Finally, Obatala built his own home in this new land of Ife and rested from his tasks.

Welcome, Yemoja!

In another time out of mind, Obatala once again grew restless. He was lonely in Ife, with only his black hen for company. One day, the great Orisa Yemoja visited. Greatly pleased by the visit, Obatala related how lonely he was. Because of his loneliness, Yemoja decided to stay with Obatala, become his wife, and live with him.

To celebrate and welcome his wife, Obatala decided to take the juice

Crafting perfect children

The next day, Yemoja and Obatala began to fashion their children. They fashioned some from the dark clay and some from the light, each child beautiful and perfect. They fashioned tall and short children, each one beautiful and perfect. They fashioned delicate children and rounded children, each one beautiful and perfect.

When the evening was done, they decided to rest from their arduous task. Both enjoyed each other's company and sipped on the

cool Emu, which had fermented. Eventually, Yemoja retired to sleep, but Obatala continued to create even more children. He would have a hundred million, so back to work he went.

Dangers of palm wine

As the night wore on and Obatala continued to labor, he grew thirsty again, and so, as he worked, he sipped Emu. Over time and without realizing, Obatala began to get drunk, yet he labored on. He fashioned some of the dark clay, some of the light, but these children were no longer so perfect, for some had short arms, while some had long. He fashioned tall and short, but these were also not perfect, for some were too tall and some too short. He fashioned delicate children and rounded children, but these, too, were not perfect for some could not talk and some could not see, yet Obatala labored on.

As the evening wore on, Obatala finally grew weary in his drunkenness. He fell into a deep, restful sleep. As the sun began to rise, Yemoja arose to greet the day with prayer. She praised Olodumare and sang a song of praise to Esu who creates all possibilities. She sang a praise song to all of the Orisa on the right and to all the Orisa on the left. She praised the earth under Ife and praised the rising sun. Finally, she implored Olodumare to give life to the children that she and Obatala had created. She prayed long and hard, unaware that, among their creations, Obatala had wrought deformity. Hearing her prayers, Olodumare breathed life into their creations and then retreated once more to the sky.

Children, perfect and imperfect

When Obatala awoke from his drunken slumber, he found himself among the many children that he and Yemoja had created, some perfect and some not so perfect. Ashamed of himself, he went off to tell Yemoja what he had wrought. With his head hung in shame, Obatala explained to Yemoja what he had done, swearing that, from that day forward, he would never again drink Emu. He swore that those who were not so perfect would be his own specially protected children. Yemoja, on the other hand, swore that she could see the perfection in each individual and would love all equally.

Yemoja and Obatala saw that their work was done. They climbed back up the golden chain, returning to their place among the other Orisa.

– IFADOYIN SANGOMUYIWA

Ejiobge

The furthest end of the road
Is hid by misty weather
Ijokun, climbing plan
Hides the forest's beauty
Thus declared Ifa
To Obatala
At the time when
The whole world,
amazed asked:

Does it require
Twenty one years
To create one albino?

Obatala replied

But this is
The flower of my creation!
Do you not understand
that the albino is
Obatala's flower?

The Goblin and the Huckster

THERE was once a regular student, who lived in a garret, and had no possessions. And there was also a regular huckster, to whom the house belonged, and who occupied the ground floor. A goblin lived with the huckster, because at Christmas he always had a large dish full of jam, with a great piece of butter in the middle. The huckster could afford this; and therefore the goblin remained with the huckster, which was very cunning of him.

One evening the student came into the shop through the back door to buy candles and cheese for himself, he had no one to send, and therefore he came himself; he obtained what he wished, and then the huckster and his wife nodded good evening to him, and she was a woman who could do more than merely nod, for she had usually plenty to say for herself. The student nodded in return as he turned to leave, then suddenly stopped, and began reading the piece of paper in which the cheese was wrapped. It was a leaf torn out of an old book, a book that ought not to have been torn up, for it was full of poetry.

"Yonder lies some more of the same sort," said the huckster: "I gave an old woman a few coffee berries for it; you shall have the rest for sixpence, if you will."

"Indeed I will," said the student; "give me the book instead of the cheese; I can eat my bread and butter without cheese. It would be a sin to tear up a book like this. You are a clever man; and a practical man; but you understand no more about poetry than that cask yonder."

This was a very rude speech, especially against the cask; but the huckster and the student both laughed, for it was only said in fun. But the goblin felt very angry that any man should venture to say such things to a huckster who was a householder and sold the best butter. As soon as it was night, and the shop closed, and every one in bed except the student, the goblin stepped softly into the bedroom where the huckster's wife slept, and took away her tongue, which of course, she did not then want. Whatever object in the room he placed his tongue upon immediately received voice and speech, and was able to express its thoughts and feelings as readily as the lady herself could do. It could only be used by one object at a time, which was a good thing, as a number speaking at once would have caused great confusion. The goblin laid the tongue upon the cask, in which lay a quantity of old newspapers.

"Is it really true," he asked, "that you do not know what poetry is?"

"Of course I know," replied the cask: "poetry is something that always stand in the corner of a newspaper, and is sometimes cut out; and I may venture to affirm that I have more of it in me than the student has, and I am only a poor tub of the huckster's."

Then the goblin placed the tongue on the coffee mill; and how it did go to be sure! Then he put it on the butter tub and the cash box, and they all expressed the same opinion as the waste-paper tub; and a majority must always be respected.

"Now I shall go and tell the student," said the goblin; and with these words he went quietly up the back stairs to the garret where the student lived. He had a candle burning still, and the goblin peeped through the keyhole and saw that he was reading in the torn book, which he had brought out  of the shop. But how light the room was! From the book shot forth a ray of light which grew broad and full, like the stem of a tree, from which bright rays spread upward and over the student's head. Each leaf was fresh, and each flower was like a beautiful female head; some with dark and sparkling eyes, and others with eyes that were wonderfully blue and clear. The fruit gleamed like stars, and the room was filled with sounds of beautiful music. The little goblin had never imagined, much less seen or heard of, any sight so glorious as this. He stood still on tiptoe, peeping in, till the light went out in the garret. The student no doubt had blown out his candle and gone to bed; but the little goblin remained standing there nevertheless, and listening to the music which still sounded on, soft and beautiful, a sweet cradle-song for the student, who had lain down to rest.

"This is a wonderful place," said the goblin; "I never expected such a thing. I should like to stay here with the student;" and the little man thought it over, for he was a sensible little spirit. At last he sighed, "but the student has no jam!" So he went down stairs again into the huckster's shop, and it was a good thing he got back when he did, for the cask had almost worn out the lady's tongue; he had given a description of all that he contained on one side, and was just about to turn himself over to the other side to describe what was there, when the goblin entered and restored the tongue to the lady. But from that time forward, the whole shop, from the cash box down to the pinewood logs, formed their opinions from that of the cask; and they all had such confidence in him, and treated him with so much respect, that when the huckster read the criticisms on theatricals and art of an evening, they fancied it must all come from the cask.

But after what he had seen, the goblin could no longer sit and listen quietly to the wisdom and understanding down stairs; so, as soon as the evening light glimmered in the garret, he took courage, for it seemed to him as if the rays of light were strong cables, drawing him up, and obliging him to go and peep through the keyhole; and, while there, a feeling of vastness came over him such as we experience by the ever-moving sea, when the storm breaks forth; and it brought tears into his eyes. He did not himself know why he wept, yet a kind of pleasant feeling mingled with his tears. "How wonderfully glorious it would be to sit with the student under such a tree;" but that was out of the question, he must be content to look through the keyhole, and be thankful for even that.

There he stood on the old landing, with the autumn wind blowing down upon him through the trap-door. It was very cold; but the little creature did not really feel it, till the light in the garret went out, and the tones of music died away. Then how he shivered, and crept down stairs again to his warm corner, where it felt home-like and comfortable. And when Christmas came again, and brought the dish of jam and the great lump of butter, he liked the huckster best of all.

Soon after, in the middle of the night, the goblin was awoke by a terrible noise and knocking against the window shutters and the house doors, and by the sound of the watchman's horn; for a great fire had broken out, and the whole street appeared full of flames. Was it in their house, or a neighbor's? No one could tell, for terror had seized upon all. The huckster's wife was so bewildered that she took her gold earrings out of her ears and put them in her pocket, that she might save something at least. The huckster ran to get his business papers, and the servant resolved to save her blue silk mantle, which she had managed to buy. Each wished to keep the best things they had. The goblin had the same wish; for, with one spring, he was up stairs and in the student's room, whom he found standing by the open window, and looking quite calmly at the fire, which was raging at the house of a neighbor opposite. The goblin caught up the wonderful book which lay on the table, and popped it into his red cap, which he held tightly with both hands. The greatest treasure in the house was saved; and he ran away with it to the roof, and seated himself on the chimney. The flames of the burning house opposite illuminated him as he sat, both hands pressed tightly over his cap, in which the treasure lay; and then he found out what feelings really reigned in his heart, and knew exactly which way they tended. And yet, when the fire was extinguished, and the goblin again began to reflect, he hesitated, and said at last, "I must divide myself between the two; I cannot quite give up the huckster, because of the jam."

And this is a representation of human nature. We are like the goblin; we all go to visit the huckster "because of the jam."

– HANS CHRISTIAN ANDERSEN *(1853)*

Taking Up the Veil

WITHIN the eclectic world of modern witchcraft, veiling, a new movement which has its roots (pun intended) in the earliest of mystical practices, is drawing numerous adherents. Veiling, the covering of the hair in order to deepen one's spirituality, was the topic of a program offered recently at the Florida Pagan Gathering, among the largest Wiccan conferences. Witches who veil offered an intriguing presentation to a standing-room-only crowd. For many contemporary witches, male as well as female, veils aren't only ritual dress, but are worn in everyday life.

Veiling probably began for practical reasons over two-thousand years ago. Nomadic tribes adopted the practice for protection against sun and dust. As communities developed, ladies kept the veil as a symbol of hearth and home. Their veils became like little houses, a kind of portable personal temple, perched on the head. This practice offered freedom of movement and showed status, while simultaneously protecting the wearer's identity. Followers of the classical Greek and Roman cults of Vesta and Dionysus would wear veils to shield the 3rd eye, maintaining purity.

Oppression and freedom

As the Abrahamic faiths (Judaism, Christianity, and Islam) made inroads, only prostitutes went bareheaded. The veil became a symbol of oppression. Eventually, many discarded the veil as a gesture of freedom. During the Middle Ages, however, the veil, along with the wimple, a high collar covering the ears and neck, was again worn for practical reasons.

Historically the need to veil comes and goes as society evolves. The gist of the message veiling conveys is assurance that one's behavior doesn't bring dishonor to either the community or oneself. Ideally, a humble and modest life and a sense of community are created by taking up the veil.

Veils offer a mysterious connection to something greater than the individual, or so wearers explain.

Brides and nuns

Saint Paul equated veils with sanctity, protection, and as an emblem of marriage. The practice of veiling was maintained by brides as they began married life, as well as by Catholic nuns, as they were married unto God. Among some Gypsies,

men and women both traditionally wear head coverings in order to protect the crown chakra and to ward off evil.

Within some tribal African spiritual traditions, a cloth head wrap, a descendant of the veil, may be worn to symbolize a crown. This is a reminder that all who wear it are royalty. The cloth can be unwound during ritual dances to symbolize leaving the mundane world behind. Veils appear in the Northern mystery circles, sometimes taken up by those who have pledged to follow Odin or Loki. Usually Nordic veils are red, the favored hue for inscribing runic spells. Red symbolizes the life's blood. It's a color of luck and high magic.

Witches who veil

Modern witches who wear the veil are drawn to a wide variety of styles, reflecting diverse spiritual traditions. Besides the Gypsy-style head scarf, a rolled turban style is popular.

Two styles tend to be favored by men. The Turkish style is a veil that covers the head, circles the throat, and then ties in the back, leaving the face exposed. The Marian veil covers the head, drapes over the shoulders, and also leaves the face bare. From the Middle East – the land of veils – comes the Hijab style, a full body veil that covers the face, either completely or partially. An ultra-thin, often beautifully embroidered second veil is worn beneath the burqa, a covering that veils the entire body.

Of course, the practice of veiling isn't always voluntary and it is controversial. Those who choose to take up the veil full time report experiencing negative reactions; so the wise will be discreet and thoughtful in deciding when and whether to begin veiling. In any case, it is very interesting to experiment. At the Florida Pagan Gathering, participants who attended the presentation about veiling were given the opportunity to try on different types of head coverings. The resulting psychological impact, changes in energy and different perceptions led to deeper insights into why veiling has suddenly developed a wider appeal among Pagans.

– DIKKI-JO MULLEN

Ganesh and the Milk Miracle
A contemporary paranormal phenomenon

IT BEGAN in New Delhi, where, during the predawn hours of September 21, 1995, a devout, but otherwise ordinary man dreamt that Ganesh, Hinduism's beloved elephant-headed god, thirsted for a drink of milk. Waking from the dream, the man rushed to a nearby temple. Although the resident priest was skeptical, he permitted the man to offer a spoonful of milk to a small statue of the deity. As both men watched in amazement, the milk vanished immediately, just as if consumed by Ganesh. That was only the beginning. What followed over the next twenty-four hours was astonishing

Word of this miracle spread at breakneck speed. The news that a statue of Lord Ganesh was drinking milk first passed locally from temple to temple, but was soon seized by the national and international news media. CNN and the BBC were among the television stations that broadcast news of the miracle. The Washington Post, The Daily Express, The Guardian and The New York Times sent journalists to investigate. All reported that the incredible event was real.

A great soul is born
Soon millions of awestruck devotees in virtually every Hindu household, temple, and shrine all over the world began to offer milk to their own statues. For twenty-four hours, Ganesh reputedly sipped this milk all up, drop by drop. A bride and groom married on that day offered Ganesh milk during their marital ceremony, requesting that he bless their nuptials. Witnesses from India to Trinidad to the United States and throughout Africa and South America testified that they saw Ganesh drink. Thousands of gallons of milk were consumed. The miracle seemingly proved that a divine force is active in our universe. Some devotees believe that the miracle indicates that a great soul – a saint – was born on that day.

Scientists, attempting to debunk this miracle, insisted that it was surface tension, capillary action, or even mere hypnotic suggestion created by mass hysteria, but they could not explain why the milk miracle had apparently never previously occurred and why it abruptly ceased just twenty-four hours after the dream.

Lord of Obstacles
Ganesh, also known as Ganesha and Ganapati, is among Hinduism's principle deities. With his benevolent expression, elephant head, and round belly, the image of Ganesh typically

146

raises a smile. His huge fan-like ears reputedly hear all pleas for his help and assistance. The snake that appears at his waist represents divine kundalini energy. Lord Ganesh represents success in all endeavors. He sweeps away obstacles, destroys evil, and brings wealth and wisdom.

Many-handed Ganesh holds a noose that snags and captures all difficulties, a goad to gently propel humanity forward, and a broken tusk that has been transformed into a pen. Ganesh is the special patron of writers. Books printed in India often feature his image on the title page. Ganesh rides a mouse, suggesting that his influence is pervasive and that he possesses the power to transcend desire.

– GRANIA LING

Jovial and benevolent, Lord Ganesh is renowned as the master of new beginnings. Chanting his mantra invokes his aid in removing all obstacles that prevent one's progress: *Om Gum Ganapataye Namaha*. Miraculous results are reported. Request that Ganesh sweep all obstacles from your path, perhaps also burning a candle or incense in his honor. Small silver spoons may also be placed on Ganesh's altar in commemoration of the miracle of milk.

Graveyard Dust

I began to feel bad, worse than I ever before
Lord, I was out one morning, found black dust all round my door

– Black Dust Blues
lyrics by Selma Davis, music by Gertrude 'Ma' Rainey

GRAVEYARD dust or graveyard dirt is exactly that: dirt taken from a grave. This dirt is considered exceptionally magically powerful, because of its associations with the dead and their proximity to the spirit world. Graveyard dirt can be a potent ingredient in a spell or mojo, but use it only when a genuine need exists. The dead prefer not to be bothered with trivial matters.

The closer the dirt was to the corpse, the more potent it is considered to be. More power can also be generated by combining the dirt with moss scraped from a fresh grave. Graveyard dirt may also be mixed with herbs, nails, sulfur, or chimney soot.

A victim's grave or a perpetrator's grave?

Graveyard dust is permeated by the character of the deceased. Spells of revenge and retribution require dust from the graves of the violent, the criminal, or, conversely, from those of victims of violence. Beware, however: such energy is dangerous. Attempting to harness it may be hazardous, especially for the inexperienced.

Spells of protection, fertility, and good fortune require dirt from the grave of a kind, generous person, especially someone who knew you and would be inclined to help you. The dirt from the grave of a parent or grandparent is especially useful in protection spells, if that person watched over you while alive. In the bleak days of slavery in the United States, some believed that if an escaping slave put dirt from an ancestor's grave in his or her shoe, the master's dogs would be unable to track him.

A midwife's grave; a healer's grave

The dirt from a healer's grave can be efficacious in healing spells. The dirt from a midwife's grave may lend spiritual aid during pregnancy or childbirth. Dirt from a lawyer's grave may aid in court cases – providing, of course, that you are on the side of justice. Dirt from a teacher's grave may assist in passing exams or learning new material.

Although the strongest, most reliable assistance comes from someone who knows you and is inclined to help, all is not lost if you are far from the graves of those who love you. In that case, locate the grave of someone you believe might be willing to assist you. Explain your situation. Introduce yourself in quiet meditation at the graveside.

Ask for aid and then request permission to take some dirt. Offer payment in the form of coins, drink, food, tobacco, or some combination. Some older traditions specify leaving pure silver coins, although these are currently challenging to obtain. If leaving a libation, consider the preferences of the deceased: a teetotaler would probably prefer a pleasant fruit punch or fine cup of tea to a hefty tipple of rum.

Midnight, during a waning moon

Dirt for malevolent spells is often gathered at midnight, during a waning moon phase. Graveyard dirt for benevolent spells may be gathered whenever it is needed. Planetary correspondences may also be incorporated when harvesting graveyard dust. For example, gather dust for success and prosperity on Sundays, whereas dust for love might be better gathered on a Friday. Avoid Tuesday, which is associated with the planet Mars, unless the dirt is intended for a vengeance spell.

For graveyard dirt to work its magic, it must come in contact with the target. If casting spells for protection, prosperity, healing, or other benevolent reasons, the easiest method is to put the dust in a small pouch, instructing the target to wear it close to the body.

Shake out your shoes

Spells of revenge or retribution tend to be secret (and you wouldn't be casting one of these without serious ethical consideration, right?), thus stealth may be required. Sprinkle the dust somewhere where the intended target will walk over it. The steps leading from the target's residence is a traditional choice, as it's assumed that the person will eventually need to leave or return home.

Of course, you run the risk of being noticed, which is why those who used graveyard dirt for justice, during times when no other justice was forthcoming, would often scatter it discreetly on a pathway or in the target's yard. Still, historically, there have been those willing to risk their lives in order to sprinkle graveyard dirt in the offender's shoes, an extremely powerful mode of administration.

– MORVEN

Edgar Allan Poe

Literary conjurer of the macabre and mysterious

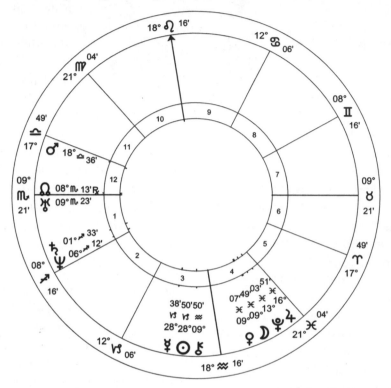

"I WISH I could write as mysterious as a cat," and the haunting echo of "Nevermore" from *The Raven* evoke the familiar literary wizardry of Edgar Allan Poe. Drama punctuated Poe's life. His birth occurred on Thursday, January 19, 1809, at 1:30 AM in Boston, Massachusetts, soon after Eliza Poe, his young actress mother, finished her evening's performance with a traveling stage troupe. His mother would die when he was just three. His father, actor David Poe Jr., had already abandoned the family.

Poe's Scorpio ascendant, with Uranus rising at exactly 9 degrees, highlights the unusual and unstable, promising a life of excitement and surprises. This particular zodiacal degree is traditionally associated with a deprived childhood fraught with danger, loss of a parent, or other relationships with adults which aren't conducive to well-being. There can also be great personal suffering rooted in bouts of depression and madness. However, the Scorpio ascendant is favorably aspected, adding brilliance and survival skills to the mix. Poe was adopted after his mother's death by a wealthy Virginian, John Allan.

Young Edgar received a good early childhood education at the Manor School in London and later returned to the United States to attend the University of Virginia. His Sun and Mercury are exactly conjunct in Capricorn (on the Aquarius cusp) in the 3rd house. This shows his keen intellect and writing ability. An inborn wealth of spiritual knowledge, a touch of melancholy, and affinity for poetry are indicated when the Capricorn-Aquarius cusp is prominent. Poe became estranged from his adoptive family after accruing gambling debts and dropping out of college. His Saturn-Neptune conjunction in Sagittarius in the 1st house squares his Pisces placements, showing a struggle with addiction. In later years his use of alcohol and opiates would be a catalyst for further trouble. However, this planetary pattern is also highly imaginative and reveals a rapport with animals, nature, and the supernatural.

In 1827 Poe's first book, *Tamerlane and Other Poems,* was published to critical acclaim, and Poe reconciled with his adoptive father, who arranged for him to attend West Point. Poe's Mars, which rules the military, is in Libra, its sign of detriment, in his 12th house, which rules loneliness and illusion. Mars is also square the natal Capricorn placements. The result was ill-fated. Poe deliberately behaved in a way which resulted in his expulsion from the military academy in 1829 and a permanent rejection by his family. At the same time he published another book, *Al Araf,* and moved to Baltimore, Maryland, where he would live for the rest of his life. Baltimore is ruled by the sign of Scorpio, in harmony with his ascendant, and it was there that his genius blossomed. Poe, one of the most prolific writers of all time, became one of the first authors to earn his living as a journalist. The Part of Fortune in Sagittarius, a sign which relates to philosophy and published writing, is in his 2nd house of earned income.

Poe's obsession with decay, madness, and death profoundly influenced the literary genres of horror and fantasy. He is credited with inventing the detective story with *Murders in the Rue Morgue.* His work is rich with curiosity, the stuff of nightmares, and elements of prophecy. Born at a New Moon, he was always ready to explore new territory. His narrative *Eureka* is a remarkable scientific and mystical essay which precipitated discoveries in astronomy by nearly a century. Jules Verne and Ray Bradbury both admit to being influenced by Poe. His cryptography studies were used many years later by the Americans during WW I in deciphering German codes.

Chiron in Aquarius in the 3rd house sextile Neptune reveals foresight. A very powerful water sign influence is present. His Scorpio placements trine the Moon, Venus, Pluto, and Jupiter in Pisces, showing visionary and intuitive potentials. His 7th house of marriage is Taurus and ruled by Venus. Venus is a part of the powerful Pisces stellium. This complex pattern points to great love punctuated by a favorite theme – the death of a beautiful woman. The

Illustration by Édouard Manet for a French translation by Stéphane Mallarmé of Edgar Allan Poe's The Raven.

quincunx aspect to the Moon Node at 8 Scorpio. Scorpio is co-ruled by Mars, which rules bites, supporting the likelihood of rabies.

Poe's mystique endures more than 150 years after his brief life ended. Five placements in cadent houses, which relate to the future, reveal that he was ahead of his time. In the nativity of a great person, prominent cadent houses often show that a lasting impression remains. In 2009, events around the globe celebrated Poe's 200th birthday. Beginning in 1949 and continuing for sixty years, a mysterious visitor dubbed "The Poe Toaster" left three roses and a half-finished bottle of cognac at Poe's grave in Baltimore every January 19. The visitor failed to appear in 2010, while fans waited for hours, shivering in the January cold, as they did every year hoping to catch a glimpse of this nameless mourner. Baltimore's ghost tours tout spectral evidence of Poe sightings.

For more information and to view the world's largest collection of Poe memorabilia, visit the Poe Museum. Located at 1914–16 East Main Street, Richmond, Virginia, it is just blocks from his first Richmond home. The museum charges a modest admission fee and schedules regular events honoring Edgar Allan Poe as "America's Shakespeare."

– DIKKI-JO MULLEN

poem "Annabel Lee" describes this, while exploring the poignant relationship Poe had with his wife, Virginia, whom he married when he was 27 and she was 13.

Edgar Allan Poe died at age 40 on October 7, 1849. His passing remains a topic of mystery and controversy. Many attributed it to Poe's lifelong alcohol and drug abuse. However, he had joined a temperance society, vowing to abstain, on August 27 of that year. There is evidence that rabies might have been the real culprit. The cusp of his 8th house, which rules the cause of death, is 8 degrees of Gemini. This zodiacal degree's keywords are violence and pain. It makes a fated

Edgar Allan Poe

*Edgar Allan Poe was born January 19, 1809
NS at 1:30 AM LMT in Boston, Massachusetts*

Data Table
Tropical Placidus House Cusps

Sun 28 Capricorn 51 – 3rd house

Moon 09 Pisces 49 – 4th house (waxing New Moon phase)

Mercury 28 Capricorn 39 – 3rd house

Venus 09 Pisces 07 – 4th house

Mars 18 Libra 37 – 12th house

Jupiter 16 Pisces 52 – 4th house

Saturn 01 Sagittarius 33 – 1st house

Uranus 09 Scorpio 24 – 1st house

Neptune 06 Sagittarius 12 – 1st house

Pluto 13 Pisces 04 – 4th house

Chiron 09 Aquarius 50 – 3rd House

N. Moon Node 08 Scorpio 29

Part of Fortune 20 Sagittarius 20 – 2nd house

Ascendant (Rising Sign) is 9 Scorpio 21

Magical Chicanery

The wisdom of four thieves

DEPENDING UPON who recounts their tale, the amazing and inspirational saga of the legendary Four Thieves occurred sometime between the fourteenth and eighteenth centuries. Their exploits reputedly took place in various parts of what are now France, Italy, and Spain. The gist of their legend is this:

When the Plague – also known as the Black Death, the bubonic plague, and Spanish influenza – ravaged the land, it decimated families, leaving barely a household without the loss of loved ones. And yet, a group of thieves seemed immune, robbing graves as well as slipping from home to home to carry off valuables, seemingly untouched by this deeply contagious sickness. The thieves strangled dying victims, all the while merrily looting and pillaging.

A life-saving plea bargain

For a long time, people were in such fear and mourning that they were indifferent to the thieves. Eventually, however, the assailants grew too bold and were apprehended in the act. A judge was so astonished by their ability to avoid illness that he offered them a deal, a sort of plea bargain. One account says it was acquittal and freedom, while another states it was to be mercifully hanged, rather than suffer the agony of being burned at the stake, in exchange for surrendering their secrets.

In any event, the Four Thieves quickly agreed and divulged the information: they had used antibacterial herbs that had been steeped in vinegar for a minimum of ten days. A cloth soaked in the mixture was tied over each thief's nose and mouth. Their clothing was doused, too. Some say the thieves also drank a bit of the vinegar.

Toulouse or Marseilles or…?

Since those long-ago days, up until the present, people swear by the Four Thieves remedy, claiming it has the power to stave off serious contagious illnesses, such as the flu. It often is remarkably effective. A Webster University study of Four Thieves Vinegar determined that the ingredients did have anti-bacterial and anti-viral qualities.

Jean Valnet (1920-1995), the renowned French aromatherapist claimed that the four thieves had been arrested near Toulouse, sometime between 1628 and 1631 and that he had the original recipe. Valnet sold small bottles of the concoction to inhale or rub on the face and hands to offset illness. On the other hand, according to the respected American herbalist, Dr. John Christopher (1909-1983) the thieves were caught in Marseilles and it was the King of France himself who gave them their freedom in exchange for their recipe, which Christopher identified as being slightly different from that offered by Valnet.

A spoonful of vinegar

Apple cider vinegar combined with raw honey is a popular modern folk remedy inspired by the Four Thieves tradition. Many claim a regular dose of vinegar and honey can enhance the immune system, promote longevity, and stave off illness.

Various recipes for Four Thieves Vinegar have appeared over the years. Be careful: some variations contain herbs which can be toxic, such as wormwood and comfrey. Here is a variation of Four Thieves Vinegar found to be very effective against chills and ills by a coven of healers in Florida in the early 21st century. It uses safe and easily obtained ingredients.

3 pints of apple cider vinegar,
   preferably unpasteurized
1 clove diced garlic
3 ounces finely chopped fresh ginger
1 teaspoon each clove, lemon peel,
   cinnamon, rosemary, rose hips, sage,
   and mint.
Optional: 1 teaspoon camphor (not synthetic camphor).

Mix all ingredients and store in a glass bottle. After two weeks strain and reserve the liquid for use. Either sprinkle a few drops on the hands and face or drink a teaspoon daily, as needed, in a glass of juice or water (adding a tablespoon of raw local honey if desired).

– ESTHER ELAYNE

The good, the bad, and the ugly

QUICK! Look out the window! Did you see it? Did you see the gnome? Chances are he was too fast for you and disappeared into the hills. Or perhaps he is still there after all, disguised as a sapling or rock, unwilling to reveal his presence. Don't feel too badly for the snub – gnomes largely eschew human contact, preferring to live their long lives quietly underground. The truth is you'll never see a gnome, unless he wants you to, unless he has judged you to be trustworthy enough to merit an audience with him. There are certainly many reasons to court the favor of a gnome, but be forewarned: a gnome is a fickle friend to have.

The good

Gnomes are notoriously good natured. Kind and compassionate, gnomes possess bigger hearts than their diminutive stature would suggest. Gnomes apply their incredible strength, speed, and resilience to helping injured animals and tending to forest vegetation. Gnomes are exceedingly knowledgeable and constantly apply their know-how to making their forest homes a better place. They can manipulate the

landscape as easily as clay, shaping shady glens and wending brooks for all the forest creatures to enjoy. Above all, gnomes are diligent; nothing is more satisfying to a gnome than settling down after a long day of hard work.

Consequently, one of the best ways to earn a gnome's favor is to facilitate his assiduousness. Try offering a hearty bowl of porridge at the end of the day. Place the porridge wherever you suspect the gnome to be living – small mounds of earth at the edge of woods are a good place to start. The gnome will appreciate the nourishment, awakening the next day refreshed and ready to work once again. If you continue the ritual on a regular basis, the gnome will come to regard you more affably and with less suspicion. Eventually, he will become your valued guardian.

A gnome in the home

Once wooed, your gnome will devote his immense energies to protecting your household. Gnomes will keep pests away, prevent food from spoiling, and perform minor household repairs. They are especially helpful in the garden, considering their enormous botanical

prowess. Gnomes may even elevate your spirits, as a gnome's good mood is said to be contagious. The better you treat your gnome, the better he will treat your home. If you have a particularly helpful gnome, consider offering more than porridge. Gnomes have an affinity for precious metals and gems: a small amount of gold or jewelry will go a long way to keeping your gnome happy. And it is imperative to keep your gnome happy.

The bad

One should be careful when courting the favor of a gnome. Gnomes are loyal and industrious, but they can also be impish pranksters, taking maniacal delight in confounding their new friends. Gnomes are fond of hiding important items, such as car keys and glasses. Just when the unfortunate victim has given up hope of ever recovering the item, the gnome will return it to the open, preferably to a spot previously searched. Another favorite trick is to use their earth-shaping tools to shave down one leg of a table or chair until it wiggles and wobbles. Any sugar packets thrust under the offending leg will be immediately removed and used to sweeten the gnome's dandelion tea. This is all very amusing to the gnome; less so to their targets.

Yet no matter how frustrating your gnome's antics may be, never utter a cross word in his direction. While it requires months and sometimes years of near constant cajoling to gain the trust of a gnome, it can all be lost in an instant. For all their virtues, gnomes possess terrible tempers that can flare at the slightest perceived insult.

Take, for instance, the poor farmer who forgot to leave his gnome's weekly porridge by the large oak tree where he made his home. The gnome was so insulted, he vowed to leave immediately and bring good fortune to some other farm. He packed all his possessions, ripping up his burrow and tearing the roots of the oak tree in the process. The tree became so unstable that, as the gnome left, he easily pushed the towering tree over – into the farmer's barn! That farmer escaped with only minor repercussions, because the insult to the gnome was passive.

Gnomes are said to punish the worst offenses by stealing and eating the offender's children! This is largely libelous rumor, however, as gnomes are strict vegetarians. When a gnome does steal a child, the child is turned into a gnome rather than into dinner. Still, it pays to stay on a gnome's good side.

The ugly

One final note: whatever you do, DO NOT insult or even question the gnome's appearance. While their grizzled features may appear grotesque to our shallow human sight, gnomes are actually quite proud of the crags and wrinkles that cover their countenances. And when your gnome introduces you to his wife, try not to grimace; her warts and pock marks make her all the more lovely to his eyes. Simply smile and say, "What a beautiful couple you two make."

– Tenebrous Rae

Moon Cycles

A New Moon rises with the Sun,
Her waxing half at midday shows,
The Full Moon climbs at sunset hour,
And waning half the midnight knows.

NEW	2015	FULL	NEW	2016	FULL
January 20		January 5	January 9		January 23
February 18		February 3	February 8		February 22
March 20		March 5	March 8		March 23
April 18		April 4	April 7		April 22
May 18		May 3	May 6		May 21
June 16		June 2	June 4		June 20
July 15		July 1, 31**	July 4		July 19
August 14		August 29	August 2		August 18
September 13		September 27	September 1, 30*		September 16
October 12		October 27	October 30		October 16
November 11		November 25	November 29		November 14
December 11		December 25	December 29		December 13

** Blue Moon   * Black Moon

Life takes on added dimension when you match your activities to the waxing and waning of the Moon. Observe the sequence of her phases to learn the wisdom of constant change within complete certainty.

Dates are for Eastern Standard and Daylight Time.

presage

by Dikki-Jo Mullen

ARIES 2014 — PISCES 2015

THE SUN, MOON, planets, and stars watch serenely over Earth, as if they know that the simple balance of peace and dignity will be restored in time. Profound changes have been in progress involving climate, political situations, and more: the past has melted into so much that is new and different.

Fierce Mars transits Libra through July 25. Justice, peace, teamwork, and balance are priorities. Benevolent Jupiter begins the year in Cancer, highlighting family values, history, and real estate until it enters Leo in mid-July, switching the focus to new leadership, forms of amusement, and the well-being of the very young. Until December 24 sober Saturn remains in Scorpio, in mutual reception with Pluto in Capricorn. Life extension, recycling, and new ways to battle crime will be accented. During late December, Saturn commences a long transit through Sagittarius emphasiz-ing higher education, foreign affairs, and religious values. The eclipses and retrogrades section offers more detail concerning the overall trends. Consult the daily moon sign calendar to make the most of the powerful lunar cycle.

The eclipse pattern is unusual this year in that the five eclipses are in five different signs: Libra, Taurus, Aries, Scorpio, and Pisces. Pioneering spirit, financial security, ecology, charitable endeavors, and paranormal phenom-ena will form a mosaic of growth and surprises.

Presage explains what all of this means to you. Start with your famil-iar sun sign. It's the most significant placement in your birth chart and shows where you find your path in life. If you know your moon and ris-ing signs, also consider those sec-tions. The moon relates to your emotional needs and memories, while the rising sign describes how you are perceived by others.

ASTROLOGICAL KEYS

Signs of the Zodiac
Channels of Expression

ARIES: fiery, pioneering, competitive
TAURUS: earthy, stable, practical
GEMINI: dual, lively, versatile
CANCER: protective, traditional
LEO: dramatic, flamboyant, warm
VIRGO: conscientious, analytical
LIBRA: refined, fair, sociable
SCORPIO: intense, secretive, ambitious
SAGITTARIUS: friendly, expansive
CAPRICORN: cautious, materialistic
AQUARIUS: inquisitive, unpredictable
PISCES: responsive, dependent, fanciful

Elements
FIRE: Aries, Leo, Sagittarius
EARTH: Taurus, Virgo, Capricorn
AIR: Gemini, Libra, Aquarius
WATER: Cancer, Scorpio, Pisces

Qualities

CARDINAL	FIXED	MUTABLE
Aries	Taurus	Gemini
Cancer	Leo	Virgo
Libra	Scorpio	Sagittarius
Capricorn	Aquarius	Pisces

CARDINAL signs mark the beginning of each new season — active.
FIXED signs represent the season at its height — steadfast.
MUTABLE signs herald a change of season — variable.

Celestial Bodies
Generating Energy of the Cosmos

Sun: birth sign, ego, identity
Moon: emotions, memories, personality
Mercury: communication, intellect, skills
Venus: love, pleasures, the fine arts
Mars: energy, challenges, sports
Jupiter: expansion, religion, happiness
Saturn: responsibility, maturity, realities
Uranus: originality, science, progress
Neptune: dreams, illusions, inspiration
Pluto: rebirth, renewal, resources

Glossary of Aspects

Conjunction: two planets within the same sign or less than 10 degrees apart, favorable or unfavorable according to the nature of the planets.

Sextile: a pleasant, harmonious aspect occurring when two planets are two signs or 60 degrees apart.

Square: a major negative effect resulting when planets are three signs from one another or 90 degrees apart.

Trine: planets four signs or 120 degrees apart, forming a positive and favorable influence.

Quincunx: a mildly negative aspect produced when planets are five signs or 150 degrees apart.

Opposition: a six sign or 180° separation of planets generating positive or negative forces depending on the planets involved.

The Houses — *Twelve Areas of Life*

1st house: appearance, image, identity
2nd house: money, possessions, tools
3rd house: communications, siblings
4th house: family, domesticity, security
5th house: romance, creativity, children
6th house: daily routine, service, health
7th house: marriage, partnerships, union
8th house: passion, death, rebirth, soul
9th house: travel, philosophy, education
10th house: fame, achievement, mastery
11th house: goals, friends, high hopes
12th house: sacrifice, solitude, privacy

Eclipses

Eclipses bring unpredictability, growth, and surprises. For those with a birthday within three days of an eclipse, a year of endings and new beginnings can be expected. There will be five eclipses this year; three are total and two partial. A total eclipse is more influential than a partial. Eclipses conjoining the Moon's north node are thought to be more favorable than those with the south node.

April 15, 2014	Full Moon Lunar in Libra, north node–total
April 29, 2014	New Moon Solar in Taurus, south node–partial
October 8, 2014	Full Moon Lunar in Aries, south node–total
October 23, 2014	New Moon Solar in Scorpio, north node–partial
March 20, 2015	New Moon Solar in Pisces, south node–total

Retrograde Planetary Motion

The illusion of retrograde or apparent backward planetary motion is created by the Earth's speed relative to the other planets. Astrologically, retrogrades are significant; they promise a change of pace.

Mercury Retrograde Cycle
Retrograde Mercury impacts technology, travel, and communication. Those who have been out of touch return. Complete old projects; revise, review, and tread familiar paths. Gemini and Virgo will be affected.

June 7–July 1, 2014
in Gemini and Cancer

October 4–25, 2014
in Libra and Scorpio

January 21–February 11, 2015
in Aquarius

Mars Retrograde Cycle
The military, sports, and heavy industry are impacted. Aries and Scorpio will be affected.

March 1–May 20, 2014 in Libra

Jupiter Retrograde Cycle
Large animals, speculation, education, and religion are impacted. Sagittarius and Pisces are affected.

December 9, 2014–April 9, 2015
in Leo

Saturn Retrograde Cycle
Elderly people, the disadvantaged, employment, and natural resources are linked to Saturn. Capricorn and Aquarius will be affected.

March 3–July 21, 2014 in Scorpio

Uranus Retrograde Cycle
Inventions, science, electronics, revolutionaries, and extreme weather are impacted. Aquarius is affected.

July 22–December 22, 2014 in Aries

Neptune Retrograde Cycle
Water, aquatic creatures, chemicals, spiritual forces, and psychic phenomena are impacted. Pisces will be affected.

June 9–November 17, 2014 in Pisces

Pluto Retrograde Cycle
Ecology, espionage, birth and death rates, nuclear power, and mysteries relate to Pluto retrograde. Scorpio will be influenced.

April 15–September 23, 2014
in Capricorn

ARIES
The year ahead for those
born under the sign of the Ram
March 20–April 19

"Adventurous and active explorer" is a perfect key phrase for this Mars-ruled cardinal fire sign. You are at your most exuberant best when leading others and encouraging the pursuit of exciting new projects. Direct, assertive, and expressive, Aries always migrates toward the action.

The vernal equinox finds repetitive patterns and loose ends impacting relationships. Mars is retrograde in your 7th house of partnerships through May 20. Look to the past if you would know the future. The habits of associates will provide valuable insights into what can be expected from others throughout the springtime. The Aries new moon on March 30 conjoins Uranus, ushering in a note of restless impatience. You will consider changes and eye new horizons near your birthday. Heed the small voice within near May Day.

May 3 – 28 Venus whirls through your birth sign. Express creative ideas and enjoy the arts. Others appreciate your company; loved ones are caring. They express admiration. During June and July several planets, including Mercury, Jupiter, the sun, and Venus, will tease your 4th house of home and heritage. While Mercury is retrograde

June 7 – July 1, visit a favorite and familiar vacation destination. A larger or more comfortable residence can be on the agenda. You will seek to improve family dynamics. An important family reunion near the summer solstice highlights the specifics. Summer's brightest days favor performing a house blessing. Sort through cherished photos and keepsakes.

On August 1 Mercury enters your 5th house and favorably aspects Uranus. You can enjoy sports and other competitive activities, as well as experiencing a turn for the better in love and romance. Mid-August through September 5 a strong Venus influence prevails. Ask others for advice and assistance. Associates will be accommodating and considerate. A hobby or creative idea can generate extra income.

September 14 – October 26 Mars influences your 9th house. This encourages higher education, travel, and spiritual studies. Your physical vitality will improve too. You are inspired to honor the autumnal equinox with a novel seasonal ritual. Decorate the altar with the brightest harvest crops. Include apples, corn, gourds, and colorful foliage. Add deep gold or crimson candles.

On October 8 the Aries full moon brings a total lunar eclipse that will affect you profoundly. Be prepared for the status quo to shift. Look forward to the next phase in your life. The specifics will come into focus during the ninety days ahead. All Hallows finds Mercury in opposition to you, a trend which lasts through November 8. Honor a two-faced theme with your Halloween costume. A mask with different faces front and back, a yin and yang, or a Jekyll-and-Hyde motif are some possibilities.

Mid-November through December 10, Venus moves through your sister fire sign of Sagittarius. This smooths over a prickly social situation. Accept and issue invitations. Late December through January 12, Mars highlights your sector of goals. Friends encourage you to consider an ambitious project. You are focused on the future. Accept a leadership role in an organization or community project. During the weeks before Candlemas, news arrives concerning a friend or coworker who has been out of touch. A broken promise is kept or a debt repaid. Be cautious about forming new commitments. Mull over offers until after February 11. There is secrecy afoot, and it's best not to take everything at face value.

By February 21 Mars and Venus in Aries will form a really fortunate grand trine in fire signs with Jupiter in Leo and Saturn in Sagittarius. Give some thought to image enhancement. Your personality and appearance are memorable. You have heightened charisma. Originality combined with energy inspires you to try new things. A significant win or achievement is very likely. The last weeks of winter are satisfying and you will accomplish much.

HEALTH

From the spring equinox through mid-July, a Grand Cross in cardinal signs aspects your sun. This indicates very high stress. You might feel overwhelmed. Take a time-out. A massage or meditation would facilitate relaxation. Jupiter, the celestial healer, enters your sister fire sign of Leo on July 17, and health gradually improves. Late winter blesses you with wellness and renewed vitality.

LOVE

The year begins with Mars making a long passage through your opposing sign of Libra. This affects your partnership sector. Someone close to you can express some frustration and the need for growth within the relationship. April 15 brings an eclipse, which ushers in change. Humor and flexibility are essential. Venus influences favor happiness in May, August, and November. Wear red for love triumphant and arrange romantic liaisons then.

SPIRITUALITY

March 20 – April 5 finds Mercury racing through your 12th house of spirituality. This supports dream work as a spiritual aid. Purchase a journal for impressions upon waking and sleeping. Invite like-minded friends to discuss the deeper meanings of dreams. Exchange thoughts about dream interpretation and lucid dreaming for further insights.

FINANCE

The April 29 eclipse in your 2nd house of finances might bring either a change in your source of income or extra expenses. Stay alert regarding new developments in your field of employment. On December 23 serious Saturn moves into a position promising much greater prosperity. This will materialize by winter's end. Dedicate Candlemas rites to monetary gain.

TAURUS
The year ahead for those
born under the sign of the Bull
April 20 – May 20

The Zodiac's sensible romantic, Taurus, is a fixed earth sign ruled by Venus. With patience, determination, and an enormous dash of common sense, you nearly always obtain what you desire. You're the one others depend upon to come through and cope when there's an important need to be met.

Spring begins with Venus brightening your midheaven. Your competence and creativity are in evidence at work. You will shine in the professional sphere through April 5; however, there is much brewing beneath the surface. By the end of April, changes develop. The specifics come to light near the time of the solar eclipse in your birth sign on April 29. Adaptability and a progressive outlook are essential. New twists and turns are developing. Mercury races through Taurus from April 24 – May 7. Beltane finds you traveling and digesting new ideas. Your beautiful voice is admired by others. You might be called upon to do some public speaking or perhaps lead a sacred May Day song or chant.

Late May through the summer solstice, Venus glides through your birth sign, attracting favors and admiration. Your standard of living and financial situation look promising at the summer solstice. Dedicate the longest of days to a ritual blessing for either love or money. The end of June through July 16 finds Jupiter completing a positive aspect in your 3rd house. This is a wonderful cycle for nurturing relationships with siblings or neighbors. Pay attention to current events then, too. Television coverage or a newspaper story offers useful insights and perspectives.

Late July – early August has Mercury, Jupiter, and the sun clustering in your 4th house of real estate and family dynamics. Home improvements, perhaps bolstered by a house blessing or Feng Shui consultation at Lammas, will appeal. Be philosophical and accepting of your family background. Release any resentment concerning the past. The important focus is on where you're going, not what's come before.

From mid-August through September 3 Mercury darts through your 5th house of leisure. Pursuing a new hobby or art project generates a joyful mood. Share this interest with a loved one. A mood of joy is pervasive. The autumnal equinox finds Mars in your 8th house, where it remains until just before Samhain. You will be especially curious about the spirit world and reincarnation. A regressive hypnosis session or a stroll through a historic cemetery could trigger a vivid past life recollection. A spirit entity brings a friendly message from the afterlife. A classic ghost costume is your ideal choice for Halloween wear.

The full moon in Taurus on November 6 ushers in a four-week cycle which emphasizes partnership and competition. Your 1st and 7th houses are strong, showing the need to balance personal needs with your obligations to others. A legal matter can be settled through compromise and negotiation. Mid-December through January 3 Venus and Mercury are favorably placed in your 9th house. Philosophical discussions and travel are extremely promising near the winter solstice. Accept an invitation to journey through the winter landscape. Shadows and the moonlight on the freshly fallen snow offer a vision of times to come.

January accents career. A Mars influence promises a competitive spirit and the need to work especially hard. At Candlemas retrograde Mercury creates some work-related confusion. Analyze repetitive patterns and verify instructions. Burn white altar candles for clarity and peace. Mid-February finds you rising above difficulties. Everything will move forward smoothly. By February 21 Mars and Venus will join Uranus in your 12th house. You'll be drawn toward charitable projects. Sharing with those less fortunate brings a sense of satisfaction. Winter's last days usher in a mood of quiet reverie. Time spent alone in contemplation will enable you to make productive plans for the future.

HEALTH

From the spring equinox through July 25 Mars passes through your 6th house of health. This brings a caution against exposure to extreme temperatures or stress. Overly demanding physical workouts or sports which carry a risk of injury should be avoided. Mars will be retrograde through May 20, showing that your past health history can be a valuable guide to making the best health choices. Your vitality improves as autumn begins.

LOVE

Your 5th house of love links with service. Often a romance begins while you're working on a worthwhile project with someone you admire. Always be careful not to be overly critical of a loved one. Balance each complaint with a compliment. Sharing your love of nature can facilitate a true love connection. June and September favor romantic interludes.

SPIRITUALITY

From spring through mid-July two spiritual indicators, Jupiter and Neptune, form a trine aspect affecting your 3rd and 11th houses. This pattern favors attending spiritual discussion or study groups with friends. Select a favorite magical text, inspirational book, or spiritual poetry to read and review. Short pilgrimages to visit sacred sites can also broaden your spiritual perspective.

FINANCE

A Saturn opposition will have a powerful influence on finances until December 24. Obligations to others and external factors can drain your resources. Use caution in acting upon financial advice that has any element of risk. Live within your means. Support loved ones with kind encouragement, but don't lend or give away the funds you may need for yourself.

GEMINI
The year ahead for those
born under the sign of the Twins
May 21–June 20

The versatile and restless Twins thrive on variety. There is a lightness about this Mercury-ruled mutable air sign. You prefer active involvement with several projects and ideas simultaneously rather than being limited to a single focus. Much is accomplished through your natural skill with the spoken and written word.

There is an effortless quality, a sense of ease, prevailing from the vernal equinox through All Fool's Day. Venus and Mars are in air signs, in a harmonious aspect which affects your sun. Enjoy games and creative activities with friends. A love connection deepens. On April 8 Mercury joins the sun in your 11th house, turning your thoughts toward plans for the future as well as humanitarian projects. Group activity sets the pace. Bless your community on May Day.

May 8 – 29 will be hectic with Mercury rushing through your birth sign. Much can be accomplished if you stay organized. A quick journey is productive near the new moon in Gemini on May 28. Finances hold your attention during the first half of June, as there is an accent on your 2nd house. It's a good time to learn more about monetary options and to correct any budgeting glitches. Just after the summer solstice, Venus enters your birth sign where it will remain until July 18. Cultural activities would be enjoyable; plan an evening at the theater or stroll through an art festival. July 2 – 31, when retrograde Mercury is over, is a wonderful cycle for vacation or educational travel.

Several planets, including Jupiter, will highlight your 3rd house from late July through August. Celebrate Lammas with storytelling or poetry recitations. This transit favors catching up on reading, letter writing, or phone calls. September finds you juggling domestic and professional responsibilities. There is a hectic pattern involving oppositions between your 4th and 10th houses. The full moon on September 8 brings the specifics into focus. Artistic expression is favored at the autumnal equinox. Take your camera along when walking outdoors to admire the colors.

October finds retrograde Mercury going back and forth in your 5th and 6th houses. Children or animal companions need your loving attention. Include seasonal fruits and vegetables in meals to facilitate good health. Toast All Hallows with fresh apple juice. A past life memory suggests a suitable Halloween costume.

Accept what seems meant to be during November and early December. Mars joins Pluto in your 8th house of mysteries, creating a fated quality. There can be a deeper awareness of the spirit world and thoughts about the afterlife. Be patient regarding investments, an inheritance, or insurance settlement. Negotiation can be necessary to obtain expected funds. The full moon in your birth sign on December 7 brings a favorable conclusion to a situation. Draw down the moon to illuminate the path leading to your brightest and best future. Mid-December showcases a partner's talents. Offer praise and support. An active quest for spiritual awakening characterizes the winter solstice. Competitive activities can open a bridge to higher consciousness as the new season begins.

By January 6 Mercury, Venus, and Mars are in your sister air sign of Aquarius. This broadens your perspective, favoring studies and travel. Mid-January is a wonderful time to get started on a writing project. By Candlemas Mercury will be retrograde; the holiday can bring last-minute changes in plans. Religious tolerance may be an issue. Keep a debate about spiritual matters cheerful and kind. Differences are resolved by February 12 when Mercury will be direct. Near Valentine's Day business and pleasure combine gracefully; the rest of the month finds coworkers friendly and appreciative. A strong fire sign emphasis makes the last weeks of winter interesting, yet hectic. There will be much correspondence to attend to. This can involve a board meeting for an organization or a convention.

HEALTH

The spring and early summer find Saturn retrograde in your health sector. There can be low vitality or a chronic health condition to correct. Patiently work toward wellness. The results of long-term lifestyle habits can be a factor. The favorable eclipse on October 23 brings a breakthrough. Efforts made at improving health begin to be more effective. After December 24, when Saturn changes signs, the health picture is much brighter.

LOVE

The full moon on April 15 brings a total eclipse in your 5th house of love. The entire year will be a time of new discovery and changing dynamics related to romance. This can take your heart's desire in a new direction or show an existing relationship in a new light. Meditate on the Lovers card in the Tarot. It has a special affinity with your birth sign and would be a good focus for a ritual to protect true love.

SPIRITUALITY

The planet Uranus has a link to your 9th house of philosophy and religion. You can change your spiritual focus periodically. Spiritual practices which allow freedom of expression and original exploration will attract you. Try drumming under the full moon on August 10 for a unique spiritual experience.

FINANCE

The lunar phases can guide you in understanding prosperity planning cycles. Moon-ruled Cancer oversees your 2nd house of finances. Jupiter, the most benevolent of planets, will be in your financial sector from the early spring until July 16. Pursue opportunities for gain then. It will be possible to repay debts and cultivate new sources of income at that time.

CANCER
The year ahead for those
born under the sign of the Crab
June 21–July 22

Strong-willed, sentimental, and acquisitive, the Crab clutches and collects all that it sees. This moon-ruled cardinal water sign is emotional and caring with a protective attitude toward everything from treasured possessions to beloved pets and people.

Springtime through mid-July finds lucky Jupiter in your own birth sign of Cancer. Jupiter is said to be exalted in Cancer, indicating that this is a most promising cycle for you. Past efforts are rewarded, and opportunities abound. Focus on your heart's desire and make the most of what the universe offers. From the vernal equinox through the first week of April, Mercury floats with Neptune to form a grand trine in the water signs. Your insights are wonderful; it's easy to learn.

The last three weeks of April through May Eve, a Venus transit brings a sweet and promising love connection. Spiritual art, music, and literature have great appeal. In May and June, Mars completes its retrograde in the 4th house of home and family. Extra attention is needed on home maintenance and family situations. Compromise with a relative to cool anger.

Near the summer solstice your 12th house is emphasized. Take time for solitary reflection to restore balance. Listen for the voices of the wind and attune to nature's rhythm at the new moon in Cancer on June 27. July 14 – 31 Mercury will transit your 1st house and conjoin your sun. This favors travel, especially along the coast or overseas. Heed facial expressions and nuances in the vocal tones of others for meaningful communication at Lammas. August accents salable job skills and money management. All month a grouping of planets in Leo, your 2nd house, reveals that you are conscientious and concerned about doing the best job possible. Others appreciate this much more than they might say.

The first half of September brings higher vitality and strength. Scorpio transits favorably aspect your sun. This is wonderful for making a success of challenges and for enjoying sports. Just before the autumnal equinox Mars enters the sector of your horoscope which rules small animals. Celebrate the autumn by installing a birdbath and feeder. A cuddly kitten or puppy seeking a home arrives before All Hallows. Adopting the new pet would bring great joy. Name it Pumpkin, Spooky, or Boo in honor of the season. A werewolf or black cat costume would be a good choice for your Halloween wear.

October 25 – November 16 Venus is in your love sector. Reveal where your heart lies to the one you would woo. Make plans to share the winter holidays together. From late November throughout December your 7th house is strong. Others set the pace and make plans which involve you. Cooperate. The winter solstice brings a surprise announcement from a companion. Bless a token on the shortest day for maintaining goodwill and camaraderie, then present it to the one you admire as the sun sets.

In January, mysteries and afterlife contacts are emphasized by 8th house transits. It's a favorable cycle for looking beneath the surface. A lost item is retrieved near Candlemas. February finds Venus in Pisces, your 9th house of faith and philosophy. Share spiritual observances with a loved one. Read magical texts together or plan a journey to visit a sacred site or a distant covenstead. Feel the presence of the Lord and Lady.

March promises greater visibility, even some recognition and renown. Venus, Mars, and Uranus are poised in your 10th house. A strong aspect from Pluto ushers in a sense of destiny. Be alert to synchronicities. The universe is offering guidance through omens and signs.

HEALTH

The springtime begins with very favorable solar aspects, promising good vitality. Follow wholesome fitness and dietary practices early in the year. Neptune, which rules spiritual and angelic healing, is prominent, so faith can have a positive affect on your well-being. By the end of December, Saturn will be in the midst of a long passage through your health sector. Be realistic and patient concerning health goals. Schedule regular check-ups during the winter.

LOVE

Your 5th house of love is very prominent from the spring through late autumn. Love prospects are especially good in April, July–August, November, and also in February. One whom you love will be encouraged by your expressive facial features, which make your deepest feelings visible at a glance. You don't have a poker face. The October 23 eclipse profoundly affects love. Either a relationship reaches a turning point, or a new romantic prospect appears suddenly and changes your life.

SPIRITUALITY

The Cancer full moon on January 4 is strongly colored by a Pluto opposition. This shows a transformative spiritual energy afoot during mid-winter. Prepare an altar to honor Pluto as well as moon goddess archetypes. A cycle will follow which could bring astral travel, shape shifting, and connections with otherworldly beings such as spirit guides and ascended masters. Keep a vigil by moonlight; wait and watch.

FINANCE

The "millionaire's aspect" is a term coined by famous 20th century astrologer Grant Lewi for the Jupiter-Saturn trine. Perhaps Lewi was being a bit colorful with his description, but this aspect does point to a comfortable lifestyle and adequate resources. From the early spring though mid-July, Jupiter in Cancer will be trine Saturn in Scorpio, affecting your financial prospects favorably. You should be able to make real strides toward a desirable financial future.

LEO
The year ahead for those
born under the sign of the Lion
July 23–August 22

The dignified Lion hunts with confidence and assurance. Sincere, expressive, and affectionate, you seek the brightest and best that the jungle of life offers. Ruled by the sun, there is always a warmth and a dramatic quality to this charismatic fixed sign of fire.

From the vernal equinox through All Fool's Day, the sun is conjunct Uranus in your 9th house. Enrollment in an interesting study program or joining a tour group headed toward an exotic destination can be on your agenda. Grandparent and grandchild interactions take on an added sparkle. The April 15 eclipse is conjunct retrograde Mars in your 3rd house. Decisions are being made regarding transportation. You might purchase a new vehicle in time for May Day. A disagreement with a neighbor or sibling can become volatile. Be diplomatic. Remember that sometimes silence is the best answer when facing a difficult individual. The confrontation runs its course if you don't fuel the controversy.

Venus affects spiritual growth during May. Mystical art, foreign language studies, and literature are sources of inspiration. Cultivate friendships with those from other lands. In June retrograde Mercury creates a stir in your 12th house. A disappointment from long ago may surface anew through a dream or memory. Don't repeat the past. Dismiss it as a learning experience and look ahead. The summer solstice is a time to focus on release.

The first half of July brings a benevolent planetary pattern in your 11th house. Friends are concerned and appreciative. Make an effort to expand your social circle while planning for the future. Community projects and humanitarian endeavors add a richness to your life. The new moon in Leo on July 26 finds you drawn to projects which make a difference in the world. You would enjoy fundraising for a charity.

On Lammas, Mercury joins the sun and Jupiter in your sign. A tropical island motif would be a good magical choice for a seasonal altar. Try using a ritual gleaned from the mysticism of Hawaii's Huna tradition. Anticipate especially colorful and exciting birthday celebrations this year. Extra calls and mail as well as travel opportunities make August very busy.

August 16 – September 22 your 2nd house of finances sets the pace. You'd benefit from brainstorming sessions about monetary options. Someone near you who knows about finance has worthwhile ideas to share. Shopping for a long-desired purchase can be enjoyable. Business travel is possible too. The autumnal equinox finds dynamic Mars in your sector of love and romance, a trend which lasts until the end of October. A challenging and adventurous companion impresses you.

Your energy level will be high, so a hike through the forest or tickets to a football game would be enjoyable.

Cardinal sign transits in your 3rd and 9th houses engage you in a lively philosophical debate or a battle of wits in October. At All Hallows your 4th house of home and family strikes a sentimental tone. Design a costume from vintage garments found in the attic and decorate with memorabilia. Mid-November through December a dear one includes you in invitations to holiday gatherings. A romantic relationship blossoms, if you reciprocate. How about sharing an evening at the theater or attending a concert of holiday music?

At the winter solstice Mars will be in opposition to your sun, a trend which lasts through January 12. Expect challenges from others. Keep the rivalry jovial. A sense of humor provides the best defense against anger. Adopt a live-and-let-live approach if dealing with difficult people. The end of January finds Mercury retrograde in your partnership sector. Those close to you will repeat established patterns. An old flame revives by Candlemas. On February 3 the full moon in Leo encourages you to make choices that let you be true to yourself. Late February through March 17 a grand trine in fire signs eases pressure. Good deeds you've done in the past are recognized. An avocation could generate extra income. The eclipse in your 8th house on March 20, just as winter draws to a close, promises a moment of truth. As winter ends, a spirit guide might visit to solve a mystery.

HEALTH

Your vitality is affected from mid-April through the autumnal equinox by retrograde Pluto in your health sector. Strive to remedy health conditions at that time. Your teeth, spine, or knees need attention. By the end of the year, favorable influences from both Jupiter and Saturn show a major turn for the better regarding health.

LOVE

On December 24 serious Saturn begins a two-year passage through your love sector. The winter ushers in a stable and long-lasting relationship built around addressing mutual needs and respect. A helpful and supportive feeling prevails as you and the one you care about work together to accomplish worthwhile goals.

SPIRITUALITY

This year's eclipse pattern impacts your spiritual direction. Prepare for some surprises related to philosophical perceptions, especially in October and again in March 2015. You might decide to reside in a spiritual retreat for a time to connect with the divine. Messages from a spirit guide or ascended master arrive, expanding your outlook.

FINANCE

The good times begin on July 17 when Jupiter, planet of bounty and blessings, begins a year-long transit through Leo. The financial outlook brightens a great deal during the autumn and winter months. Near your birthday a way to recoup a past loss will become available.

VIRGO
The year ahead for those
born under the sign of the Virgin
August 23–September 22

Holding her ripened sheaf of grain, the practical Virgin waits for the right moment to complete the harvest. Purity, planning, precision, and perfect timing characterize Mercury-ruled Virgo. As a mutable earth sign you have an affinity with the land.

The vernal equinox arrives with a scattered, distracted note. Mercury is opposing your sun and conjunct evasive Neptune. Verify appointments and instructions; keep receipts and records in order. On April 7 a Venus influence comes to the rescue. Throughout the rest of April others are sensitive and helpful. A partner's accomplishments merit your praise and support. A sense of teamwork prevails and your workload lightens by May Day.

May 2 – 20 your 9th house is highlighted. You're aware of how much there is to learn. Faraway shores beckon. You are attracted to travel. Exploring new ideas is an appealing prospect as well. During June retrograde Mercury brings a focus on resolving career issues. It might be time to return to a position you did well with in the past. At the summer solstice Venus is in Taurus and forms a wonderful aspect to your sun. Devote sabbat rites to honoring nature. How about a ritual blessing of your garden or making an ecology charm to protect the environment? July 1 – 25 Mars completes a transit through your 2nd house of finances. This ends frustration and touches of anger regarding the budget and cash flow.

By August the overall pressure dissipates and you'll feel more secure. Remember to offer a thank you to the Lord and Lady for all that you have at Lammas. Relax to allow guidance to come as you meditate on the sunset. The new moon in Virgo on August 25 brings a renewed sense of purpose. Select your goals for the year to come as your birthday nears. Mid-August through September your 1st house is accented. Focus on developing your skills; stay on top of new developments in your areas of expertise. Honor loyalty and embrace patriotism at the autumnal equinox.

During October Mars creates a stir regarding home and family life. Concentrate on making positive changes in living arrangements. A lighthearted, good-humored attitude during the retrograde Mercury of October 4 – 25 smooths over difficulties. A "black sheep" relative or a difficult neighbor returns and repeats negative patterns. This creates a bit of unwelcome drama. A mild response on your part diffuses the situation. The October 23 eclipse brings a change for the better.

From All Hallows through November, Mars joins Pluto in your 5th house of romance and pleasure. Invoke the Camelot tradition in choosing your Halloween costume and become your favorite character from King Arthur's court. Prepare a love philter to share with your beloved and bake sweet treats for the Samhain table. December begins on a hectic note with mutable sign squares from several planets to your sun. Prioritize and release stress through meditation, yoga, or a walk outdoors, perhaps with a beloved pet. Appreciate seasonal changes.

On December 11 Venus crosses into your sister earth sign of Capricorn; Mercury follows on December 17. Your creative ability comes in handy in making gifts and completing projects in preparation for the winter solstice. On the shortest of days you will feel restless. Get some fresh air. A day out would be uplifting.

January accents your 6th house of health. Schedule routine checkups and plan a wholesome menu. Wearing comfortable, weather-appropriate clothing will do much to assure wellness. At Candlemas light tapers of blue and white to facilitate healing. January 21 – February 11 retrograde Mercury offers valuable insights concerning health needs. This enables you to make needed changes regarding fitness. The end of February finds Venus, Uranus, and Mars in your 8th house. This brings all that has been hidden to light. It's a perfect time to connect with a spirit loved one and to review old journals and letters.

The full moon in Virgo on March 5 finds you evaluating how associates are affecting you. Seek a healthy balance between sharing with others and taking care of yourself. Late winter is an optimum time to focus on your image.

HEALTH

All year, Uranus, ruler of your health sector, will be in pioneering and progressive Aries. This favors trying new and innovative types of wellness care. At the same time, don't be overly aggressive with any treatment programs; go slowly if any risk factors are involved. The full moon on August 10 falls in your 6th house of health. That marks a time for attuning to your body, the temple of your spirit. Ask yourself what you need to stay healthy.

LOVE

A bright cycle for love occurs September 6 – 29, when Venus is in Virgo. There is an eclipse in your 7th house of commitments on March 29, 2015. Expect surprises and revelations about a relationship. Welcome growth; whatever changes are developing regarding love will be for the best.

SPIRITUALITY

Neptune, the spiritual planet, will oppose your sun all year. This makes mystical and intuitive people appear in your life. Discuss dreams, visions, and spiritual studies with others to facilitate your own spiritual awakening. At the same time, honor your own ideals.

FINANCE

The April 15 eclipse falls in your 2nd house of finance. This ushers in a series of changes which will unfold all year regarding established financial patterns. A new job or different financial strategies can manifest. The autumn months bring financial gain.

LIBRA
The year ahead for those
born under the sign of the Scales
September 23–October 23

Impartial and balanced, the Scale seeks truth through harmony. This cardinal air sign, ruled by Venus, honors beauty. Gracious, sociable, and charming, you value companionship and teamwork.

The vernal equinox greets you with challenges and action. Mars, which is retrograde, is in the midst of a long passage over your sun, lasting until July 25. Your energy level is high and you're very motivated. The Libra full moon on April 15 brings a total eclipse in your birth sign. Old patterns are shifting. A move of some type is brewing. Be flexible and observant. April 29 – May Day a strong Taurus influence in your 8th house accents insurance, investments, and other financial matters. Include prosperity blessings in Beltane festivities. May favors releasing earth-bound spirits. Encourage entities to move to higher dimensions. Light a bright yellow candle and ring a bell to accomplish this.

June finds Jupiter and retrograde Mercury in Cancer, your 10th house of career. Your efforts are rewarded near the time of the summer solstice. The way is clearing for you to realize a cherished, long-term goal. When the sun is high overhead on the longest of days, visualize the bright, warm daylight surrounding you with success. June 24–July 18 Venus moves through Gemini, your sister air sign, and creates a joyful influence in your 9th house. It's a perfect time for long-distance travel, deep philosophical studies, or writing for publication. Over the Independence Day holiday a memorable gathering of in-laws, friends, grandparents, and/or grandchildren brings joy. Take photos and assemble a keepsake album.

At the end of July, Mars joins Saturn in your 2nd house to set the pace until mid-September. The drive to work hard, acquire desired possessions, and realize financial goals motivates you. Patience is rewarded. At Lammas, identify worthwhile values. August 13–September 5 benevolent influences from Venus and Jupiter in Leo, your 11th house, bring support from friends and organizations. You will realize how highly esteemed you are by your colleagues. September is a good time to make decisions and plans, as Mercury will be racing through Libra. Travel, meetings, and preparing schedules will all progress. You are able to multitask with ease.

At the autumnal equinox reflect upon the significance of time. Bless a favorite calendar, clock, or watch to use as a charm. The September 24 new moon in Libra brings loose ends together. You are focused. October begins with Venus entering Libra, accenting your 1st house. This upbeat transit lasts until October 23. Splurge on new finery for your birthday. Your appearance reflects how others see you and how you feel about yourself. It's a productive time to seek favors and advice from helpful people. At All Hallows your 2nd house is strong. Keepsakes and collectibles added to your altar enhance the meaning of this sacred celebration. Elegant, all-black attire, perhaps including a cape, and a pin or ring featuring a skull motif would be a good costume idea.

Home improvements are at the top of your agenda. December finds Venus and Mercury moving through the home and family sector. A domestic situation is successfully resolved near the winter solstice. On the year's shortest day open windows and doors to let a breath of cold wind blow through. This will clear the premises of any negativity.

January and early February your love sector is blessed by several planets in a favorable aspect to your sun. There is time for pleasure and recreation. A romance unfolds beautifully. Children are a source of joy. The new moon on January 20 brings the specifics into focus. At Candlemas devote sacred rites to rekindling the flame of a lost love or invoking the spirit of creativity. On February 3 the full moon is conjunct Jupiter in your 11th house of aspirations. Emotional fulfillment comes from involvement in community life or an organization. You are absorbed in making future plans.

March emphasizes the 6th house. There is a vague agitation present; seek to discover and release the source of stress. You'll experience deeper psychic rapport with pets. Pay special attention to interpreting dreams about animals near the time of the eclipse on March 20.

HEALTH
Throughout spring and early summer Mars is prominent in your 1st house. Avoid sunburn hazards, confrontations, or extreme sports through July 25. A shamanic journey to connect with an animal spirit for health-related information or a spiritual healing would be successful in September or March.

LOVE
March 21 – April 5 finds Venus making a wonderful aspect for sharing cultural interests, such as music, with a loved one. The October 8 eclipse impacts your 7th house of relationships. Allow a partner to go through growth and changes. Be flexible. At the autumnal equinox or All Hallows perform magical workings to bless and protect a relationship.

SPIRITUALITY
A quincunx aspect from mystical Neptune shows that the Fates are active in your life all year. Heed what the universe is indicating through omens and signs. What seems meant to be? What just isn't coming together? Attune to synchronicities and you will receive spiritual guidance.

FINANCE
Saturn, the heavenly taskmaster, has been in your financial sector for the last couple of years. You've had to patiently cope with some budget restrictions. This austere trend ends on December 24. The late winter brings much brighter financial prospects.

SCORPIO
The year ahead for those
born under the sign of the Scorpion
October 24–November 21

Intense belief combined with faith characterizes the always mysterious Scorpion. Deeply emotional, determined, and private, this fixed water sign is co-ruled by Mars and Pluto. You welcome each ending as a new beginning, a rebirth, and new life.

Mercury dances with Neptune in good aspect to you during the first two weeks of spring, bringing a bright and cheery outlook. Write a love letter at the vernal equinox. Surprise the one you secretly admire by delivering it on All Fools' Day. Your speech and writing has a poetic and persuasive quality. The eclipse on April 15 highlights your 12th house. Memories impact you. Freedom comes through self-analysis. The last three weeks of April bring a very upbeat Venus trine. Creative expression helps you to cope with inner conflicts. Try your hand at art, music, or design. Use the chakra colors on your May Day pole or Beltane altar to elevate your focus and invoke spiritual balance.

The full moon in Scorpio on May 14 ushers in a four-week cycle of expanded awareness through travel and philosophical studies. Visiting the waterfront brings inspiration. Your perceptions and hunches are worthwhile. During June Venus moves through your 7th house of relationships. You'll take pride in the achievements of a partner or team member as the summer solstice approaches. Plan a surprise victory or appreciation party to brighten the shortest night.

A grand trine in the water signs of Cancer, Pisces, and Scorpio is in effect throughout July. Responsibilities will be less burdensome. Health and vitality are in peak form. If you have wanted to try a new career or chase a rainbow to find a long-sought prize, now is the time to move forward. At Lammas break bread and sprinkle it with sacred salt in appreciation for all that you have been given. Throughout August until September 13 Mars will be in Scorpio. This is fiery and volatile. It can be very good if used positively, but destructive if uncontrolled. Keep your temper; no one else wants it. Make constructive changes, yet avoid overkill. Get enough rest and pace yourself.

The pressure lessens at the autumnal equinox. Your 12th house, representing peace and reverie, is highlighted, allowing you to enjoy a reprieve. On October 23 a solar eclipse in Scorpio heralds surprises and thrusts you back into the action. As your birthday nears you'll be preparing for a move or a new focus in life. Others seek you out. Go out of your way to be helpful. Good deeds will be appreciated and favors returned. All Hallows finds both of your ruling planets, Mars and Pluto, in earthy Capricorn. Incorporate sacred earth into your magical workings. For your Halloween costume an earth

176

elemental such as a brownie, gnome, or troll would work well. The Green Man and Mother Nature are other possibilities.

November finds Mercury, the sun, and Saturn in your birth sign. Conversations will focus on serious issues. A business trip is meaningful and revealing. December is all about finances, as your 2nd house is prominent. A Venus influence brings loving concern toward those less fortunate. You'll offer gifts of money or practical items. Honor survival at the winter solstice; add fragrant evergreens to the altar. Serve seeds, nuts, and dried fruits at a sabbat feast on the longest night. Burn bayberry candles to assure prosperity.

January begins with a strong fire sign influence. Your 2nd, 6th, and 10th houses are involved. This makes you competitive when it comes to career, accomplishment, and status. Focus on accepting the lot fate has dealt you. There are some who have been given less, others more. You must be who you are, do what you can, and want what you have in order to be happy. By Candlemas Venus will activate your love sector. Decorate the altar with hearts and red roses. Serve chocolate and burn red and pink candles. By Valentine's Day the love and passion planets, Venus and Mars, are conjunct in your 5th house of romance, making a happy love connection. True love is paramount during the last weeks of winter. The eclipse on March 20 awakens you to what the love situation means for your long-term future.

HEALTH

April 8 – 23 a Mercury transit in your health sector turns your thoughts toward well-being. A massage to help your circulation would be a great investment in maintaining wellness early in the spring.

LOVE

On April 29 an eclipse in your 7th house marks a turning point in an existing partnership. The March 20, 2015, eclipse in your 5th house of romance brings sparkle and surprise to matters of the heart. It's an emotional roller coaster this year; look on love as an adventure. There are surprises in store.

SPIRITUALITY

The spring and early summer months find Jupiter in Cancer in your 9th house of higher consciousness. Your intuition will be especially good then. Heeding it will play a role in spiritual awakening. Enjoy seascapes, photos of the water, and recordings of waves or waterfalls to facilitate spirituality.

FINANCE

Your 2nd house of finance is ruled by Sagittarius and Jupiter. This shows that staying informed about the larger financial picture, such as worldwide financial cycles and patterns, can help you reach your own financial goals. After December 9, when Jupiter goes retrograde, you will have insight concerning the impact of old financial habits and past decisions. December – March is a good time to pay off any bills or debts.

SAGITTARIUS
The year ahead for those
born under the sign of the Archer
November 22–December 21

A zest for life characterizes this mutable fire sign. You are a restless wanderer on a never-ending quest, always targeting new goals and thriving on challenges. Ruled by jovial and optimistic Jupiter, Sagittarius can't resist being somewhat of a gambler and game player.

From the vernal equinox through the end of April financial decisions are emphasized. A Jupiter-Pluto opposition affects your earnings and investments. Use discretion in acting upon the financial advice of another. Shop for the best price on costly purchases. On May Eve offer a prosperity blessing for your workplace or a business partnership.

May 3–28 Venus joins Uranus in your love sector. This trend points to very interesting romantic connections. There's an electrical quality concerning love; your needs and desires are both changeable and intense. The full moon in Sagittarius on June 12 illustrates the need for cooperation. Networking and enlisting support from others will assure success near the summer solstice. Celebrate the longest day by offering keepsakes to those whom you depend upon and cherish. Show how much you care.

During July Mars completes a transit through your 11th house. It's time to define goals and finalize priorities if you've been multitasking. You might find yourself listening to different sides of the same story regarding conflicts. Assume the role of mediator or peacekeeper. The new moon on August 26 brings new interests. You're bored by stale situations. From August 1–15 Mercury races through Leo, your 9th house. At Lammas prepare a travel charm or make decisions about an educational program. Your horizons are expanding. The last half of August finds the benevolent planets Venus and Jupiter in a favorable aspect to your sun. This is a highly refined influence. Quality, cultural pursuits, and elevated standards will guide you. You will treasure all that is beautiful and desirable.

September 1 – 13 finds Mars and Saturn in your 12th house. You will relish peace and privacy. Be diplomatic, if a loved one accuses you of aloofness or secrecy. Consider future options and the times to come, as the autumnal equinox approaches. Mars blazes through your birth sign in October bringing excitement and challenges. Enjoy exercise; you're very motivated and can accomplish much, but keep things in perspective if there's a difference of opinion brewing. A confrontation could get out of hand, especially near the eclipses on October 8 and 23. At All Hallows Mercury highlights your 11th house. Much can be learned from a friend. Enjoy a gathering at Halloween. A safari or sailor look would be a good costume selection.

A potent water sign influence in early November finds you dwelling on old times, especially your childhood. Contact family or friends with whom you've been out of touch. On November 17 Venus enters Sagittarius. A happy cycle begins and extends through mid-December. Plan holiday travel and accept all invitations. Social contacts can have a positive impact on career growth. At the winter solstice your money sector is prominent. Bless a coin minted in your birth year as a good luck charm. As December ends you will focus on realities and practical considerations. Make a New Year's resolution to live within your means.

January finds Jupiter, your ruler, in opposition to several Aquarius transits, including Mercury and Mars. Use care in negotiations; it will take an effort to attain a meeting of the minds. Be a good listener and ask questions to clear confusion. Consider carefully and call ahead if you are thinking about travel. Avoid an expensive wild goose chase. Light a unity candle at Candlemas, with your taper joining that of a partner over the wick of a large candle. This symbolizes a common focus. The full moon on February 3 marks the start of a cycle of improved rapport with others. Valentine's Day finds you celebrating with a group of friends, perhaps attending a wedding party.

On February 21 Venus joins Mars and Uranus in Aries, your 5th house of love and creativity, ushering in a playful mood. The rest of the winter favors using your imagination and expressing original ideas. Romantic interludes hold the promise of happiness, too.

HEALTH
The new moon in your birth sign on November 22 brings insight concerning health needs. Be honest with what you already know about your body. Make dietary and lifestyle choices which will facilitate healing. This year resist the temptation to skimp on sleep or push the limits of your physical strength. A grand trine in fire signs late February – March 2015 promises improved health.

LOVE
Romance is a dramatic adventure this year, highlighted by surprise endings and beginnings. The springtime brings a hint of what is to come on March 30 when the new moon conjoins Uranus in your love sector. On October 8 a total eclipse in your 5th house of romance brings new perspectives and choices regarding matters of the heart. There is a happy ending after Valentine's Day.

SPIRITUALITY
Spiritual growth will accelerate when Jupiter enters your 9th house of higher consciousness in July. It remains there for a year. Academic studies focused on faith and religious practices around the world would be a great tool for enhancing spirituality.

FINANCE
Saturn, ruler of your 2nd house of finances, enters your birth sign in December where it will remain for several years. Patience, steady effort, and living within your means will provide the path to security. Develop a stable financial foundation. Build upon established contacts.

CAPRICORN
The year ahead for those
born under the sign of the Goat
December 22–January 19

The discriminating Goat climbs to high ground, surveying surroundings to determine the most prudent course of action. Ruled by serious Saturn, this trustworthy cardinal earth sign has an industrious and executive quality. Your knack for getting the important things done with flair wins you respect and admiration.

The vernal equinox promises to be interesting and active. A cardinal cross involving Mars, Jupiter, Pluto, and Saturn affects the angular houses of your birth chart. You are juggling household needs, career, and a relationship while honoring your own personal quest. Multitasking keeps all progressing smoothly. Late March through early April brings a good Mercury influence. A partner offers wise insights during a brainstorming session and progress is made. The sun clusters with planets in your sector of home and family life in mid to late April. New appliances, technology, and gadgets have the potential to make home life brighter, more efficient, and enjoyable. By May Day a favorable combination of planets in Taurus shifts the focus to outdoor activities. Honor Beltane by planning a camping trip or working in the garden.

May 29 – June 23 Venus brightens your 5th house of love and pleasure. It's time to enjoy sports or hobbies. Love prospects are bright too. At the summer solstice your creativity blooms. Compose a poem, write a song, or design a piece of art to delight the one you hold dear. July brings an awareness of how others depend upon you. Interesting people initiate conversations; listen carefully. A compliment surprises and pleases you near the Capricorn full moon on July 12. On July 20 Saturn turns direct. Old barriers dissolve so you can focus on the future.

August opens with Jupiter and the sun affecting your 8th house. This is wonderful for a shamanic journey to explore other dimensions, altered states, or a past life. At Lammas attend a drum circle or fire ceremony. Burn sage and cedar as a sacred smudge. Mid-August through early September transits in your 9th house favor travel and enrollment in educational programs. New information filters in, facilitating a more sophisticated outlook.

On September 6 Venus enters your sister earth sign of Virgo, where it will radiate joy through September 29. Friends share provocative ideas. Consider joining a library book club or picking up the latest best-sellers. At the autumnal equinox find an excerpt to read aloud from a classic novel or poem in honor of the fall.

The October 8 eclipse finds you thinking of home improvements, possibly even a residential move. Mid-October accents your 10th house of career. A colleague offers uplifting insights about your professional aspirations. Arrange your work space so it's more attractive and comfortable. By All Hallows Mars will be in your birth sign, where it will remain until December 4, blessing you with energy and motivation. Prepare a ritual fire circle outdoors to honor Samhain. For your Halloween costume, go with a warrior, martial arts, or chieftain look.

November through early December dynamic Mars conjoins Pluto in your 1st house. Competition exhilarates you, and your enthusiasm impacts others. Exercise is rewarding; focus on physical fitness. Mid-December through January 3 Venus will transit your birth sign. Romance brightens the short, dark days. On December 21, the winter solstice, the new moon falls in Capricorn. This initiates a better cycle regarding love. During late December you will find solace in charitable undertakings.

January emphasizes more practical considerations. Your sector of cash flow and security is accented. Seek bargains when shopping. A gift of money arrives in a birthday card. February finds Venus, Mars, and Neptune in your 3rd house in a sextile aspect to your sun. A short, impromptu journey at Candlemas is worthwhile. Your eloquent words are rich with sincere emotion and will easily sell your viewpoint to others. A conflict is resolved favorably by February 20.

March finds Saturn turning retrograde in your 12th house. Relish hours spent alone or with a small group of loved ones. Winter's end offers omens from nature. Collect a fallen feather; note a fleeting glimpse of eye contact with a deer or rabbit. Turn your face to welcome a balmy breeze.

HEALTH
Mercury makes two significant passages through your 6th house of health: May 8 – 29 and again June 18 – July 13. This makes new and valuable information about health care available. The new moon on May 28 highlights the specifics. Research wellness programs which seem suitable for you from May through mid-July. A visit to a spa would be healing and rejuvenating.

LOVE
During the spring and early summer, relationships will be blessed by benevolent and expansive Jupiter in your 7th house of partnerships. This might mean either the strengthening of an existing commitment or the arrival of a rewarding new situation with the potential for genuine romantic bliss.

SPIRITUALITY
Mystical Neptune is in the midst of a long passage through your 3rd house. Spiritual classes and discussion groups would facilitate a gradual but profound awakening consciousness. Regular work with Tarot or the runes would bring great spiritual progress.

FINANCE
From July 22 – December 22 Uranus, ruler of your 2nd house of finances, will be retrograde. Observing repeated patterns leads the way to financial success at that time. Jupiter will be favorably aspected to Uranus during the winter months. This promises a windfall which could come in the form of an investment, insurance settlement, or as a gift.

AQUARIUS
The year ahead for those
born under the sign of the Water Bearer
January 20–February 18

The congenial attitude of this fixed air sign, co-ruled by Uranus and Saturn, assures that they never lack for company. Intelligent, original, and compassionate, you will work tirelessly to improve conditions for all of humankind. New ideas pour freely from the Water Bearer's far-reaching mind in the quest for knowledge and truth.

The vernal equinox arrives amid a pleasant Venus transit through your 1st house. Love, the fine arts, and a comfortable lifestyle surround you. On April 15 a total eclipse conjoins Mars in Libra, creating a stir in your 9th house. New philosophical concepts change your spiritual outlook. Plans regarding travel and study move in a new direction. Keep a sense of good-humored tolerance if an in-law, grandparent, or grandchild generates controversy or conflict.

Trusting your intuition and unleashing your creativity leads to monetary gain during late April, when a favorable planetary pattern affects Neptune in your financial sector. The first week of May finds Mercury conjoining the sun in your 4th house. It's time to relax quietly at your own hearth. Celebrate May Day at home, perhaps erecting a maypole in your own backyard. Festoon it with ribbons in white, blue, and purple. On May 8 Mercury begins a long passage in Gemini, your sister air sign. This brings a positive mental outlook which lasts through late May and repeats again from June 18 through mid-July. Your thoughts focus on hobbies, recreation, and vacation plans. Plan a romantic and sentimental journey with a loved one near the summer solstice or over the July 4 holiday.

In late July, Mars transits your midheaven, affecting your career sector. You'll feel ambitious and competitive. At Lammas bless your professional aspirations by wearing a golden token and calling upon the power of the sun to let you shine. The Aquarius full moon on August 10 brings positive attention your way. A promotion is likely before the autumnal equinox. Mercury will trine your sun September 3 – 27 and October 11 – November 8. Writing, teaching, and public speaking are favored. Near All Hallows Venus will join Saturn and the sun to square your birth sign. Balance responsibilities and meet obligations before undertaking a new adventure. Late October through early November is not a good time to renege on a promise. Go for a cozy and comfortable look on Halloween. Resurrect your favorite hippie jeans and add a colorful sweatshirt and beads.

A favorable 11th house influence is activated from mid-November through December 10. Friends include you in holiday revelry. Future projects are discussed. As the winter solstice approaches, Mars conjoins your sun. This brings a dash of fiery enthusiasm. You will keep active through January 12. The short, cold days are brightened by planning a really full schedule of merry-making. Enjoy winter sports.

Early January – March 12 Mercury transits Aquarius, and retrograde Mercury is in force at Candlemas. Select heirloom candlesticks and hand-dipped tapers to create a nostalgic mood for the holiday altar. News from long-lost friends arrives. Your intellectual energy is strong. You figure out strategies and assimilate new information with ease. Travel and writing are favored through the winter.

During February your financial sector is emphasized. Study the budget near your birthday. Venus, Mars, and Uranus will all gather in your 3rd house March 1 –17. You'll be juggling several projects simultaneously. Try not to get distracted. Feeling overwhelmed? Ask a neighbor to extend a helping hand. The total eclipse on March 20, 2015, brings a new twist regarding security issues. Factor in the changing economic climate around you.

HEALTH

Jupiter, the zodiac's healer, is in your 6th house of health and diet during the spring and early summer. The wellness outlook is favorable. Seasonal herbs and spring vegetables are excellent menu choices. An animal companion comforts you with its healing presence. The full moon on January 4 is in your health sector and brings deeper insight regarding health considerations.

LOVE

Your 5th house of love has a mercurial quality. Discussing romantic feelings and relationships helps nurture tender affections. Friendship and love are interchangeable in your heart and mind. Make certain that you and your intended are compatible with one another's friends. Sharing jokes or online social networking gives your romantic aspirations a boost. On July 17, Jupiter enters your 7th house for a 12-month stay. This brings really promising marriage and commitment prospects your way during the rest of the year. An old heartache heals, allowing you to move forward.

SPIRITUALITY

The April 29 eclipse favorably aspects Neptune, the spiritual indicator. Your 4th and 2nd houses are affected. This encourages attunement with the spiritual energies emitted by metals, gems, and cherished symbolic keepsakes or collectibles. Dedicate a corner of your home as a spiritual retreat. This year brings a balance between spiritual values and tangible material needs.

FINANCE

The autumn and winter months are highlighted by an opposition between Jupiter, the planet of wealth, and your sun. Consider the financial suggestions offered by associates, but do make your final decisions in harmony with your own instincts. A business partnership with a friend could be worthwhile. Those who are doing well financially can indirectly have a helpful impact on your own monetary situation.

PISCES

*The year ahead for those
born under the sign of the Fish*
February 19–March 20

An aversion to struggle characterizes the gentle Fish. Your sensitivity lets you reflect the world around you with compassion and empathy. As a mutable water sign, your emotional life is active; you are always responsive. Pisces is co-ruled by Neptune and Jupiter.

Early spring finds Mercury well aspected to both Jupiter and Neptune. Expression of creative ideas, travel, and study are favored. Try visualization and spoken affirmations to materialize a cherished wish at the new moon on March 30. A Venus passage through Pisces April 6–May Eve brightens your life regarding both love and money. Plan a dance party for Beltane and decorate with flower garlands. Your hospitality will charm and impress the right people.

During May and early June Mars completes its retrograde in your 8th house. Your awareness of the afterlife and reincarnation deepens. You can find yourself deeply embroiled in research and secrets. Use discretion in acting upon the financial suggestions offered by another. Avoid either lending or borrowing significant amounts of money.

Late June through July emphasizes family life. At the summer solstice reflect upon your heritage. A pretty potpourri of seasonal herbs and fragrant blossoms would be a good way to bless your residence. By July 20 Venus will brighten your 5th house of love. The beautiful summer days hold the promise of romantic bliss. Your vitality will improve from mid-July through the end of August. A picture or plaque featuring the sun would provide an excellent focus for a health-related meditation at Lammas. Several planets, including Jupiter, impact your health sector this summer. Draw upon the healing and life-giving qualities of sunlight. Be aware of how temperature impacts your comfort and well-being.

Mars joins forces with Saturn in your 9th house throughout August and early September. Respecting diversity is essential. Your life will be touched by cultural differences. The autumnal equinox reminds you of endings and beginnings. Consider a rebirthing meditation. The fall is a time to both cherish the miracle of life and honor the mysteries of death. October finds you more competitive than usual. Mars will square your sun, bringing a fiery mood to your career sector. You will express more authority and will revel in opportunities to address challenges.

At All Hallows the pressure winds down, as Mars joins Pluto in your 11th house. You will find that others want to cooperate and share plans for the future. An otherworldly look, as an angel or alien, is a Halloween costume idea. In November Neptune gradually finishes a retrograde cycle in your 1st house. You have been polishing your skills, working on your image, and taking care of old obligations. From November 17 through the end of the year it will be easier to move forward unencumbered.

December finds Venus, Mercury, and the sun crossing your 10th house. You will be highly visible, receiving compliments on past good deeds. A promotion or award comes as a welcome surprise near the winter solstice. On the longest of nights, by the light of a burning Yule log, list your talents and accomplishments in your Book of Shadows. Draw a favorite spiritual symbol, perhaps a pentagram, at the bottom. Press a sprig of evergreen for endurance between the pages.

At the end of December Saturn changes signs, an influence which will set the pace through the winter. Your aspirations are lofty and your goals ambitious. Those older or younger will seek your help. In January your 12th house is highlighted by several planets including Mercury. You will not want to appear vulnerable. Don't disclose a confidence. Power shared is power lost.

January 28 – February 20 Venus transits Pisces, marking a time of happiness. Social activities and fine arts events are part of the party. Include ceremonial music in Candlemas rites. Light an artistically arranged candle garden. The financial picture brightens near your birthday. February 21 through late March brings a gathering of planets in your 2nd house of cash flow. A quick response to monetary opportunities which arise would help you to make the most of this. The very last day of winter, March 20, brings a total eclipse in Pisces. Prepare for a surprise. The foundation of your life whirls and twirls. Hold on for the ride; release the past. All will be well if you embrace change.

HEALTH
Jupiter, your co-ruler, will enter your health sector in July. Wellness improves throughout the rest of the year. Sun-ripened fruits and vegetables are especially nourishing. Dine alfresco in order to be nourished by nature's energies as you eat.

LOVE
The two most benevolent planets, Venus and Jupiter, will circle hand-in-hand through your 5th house of love in the springtime. Invite the one you care for to tour Paris in April or to Washington, DC to view the cherry blossoms. Express your heartfelt sentiments with a beautiful May Day bouquet.

SPIRITUALITY
The full moon on September 8 and the new moon on March 20, 2015, are both in Pisces and will both conjoin Neptune, the cosmic gateway to spirituality. Welcome higher consciousness at those times through interpreting a dream. Enjoy relaxing hypnosis or a guided meditation.

FINANCE
The eclipse on October 8 affects your 2nd house of finances. A change in your source of income is likely then. Stay in tune with new financial trends. Be progressive. Study innovative developments in your field of expertise.

Sites of Awe

Niagara Falls

IT IS IN THE AFTERNOON when my partner and I reach the parking lot near the Falls. From the car, I can hear a thunderous sound – a deep roar that seems to surround me from all directions. I can see people lined up along the edge of the parking lot. Cameras are flashing and people are posing in front of the Niagara River, which flows from Lake Erie to Lake Ontario – two of the fresh water lakes which are part of the Great Lakes of North America. Niagara Falls is actually made up of three waterfalls: the American Falls, the Horseshoe Falls, and the Bridal Veil Falls. As I rush to the rail and look over the edge – I gasp!

I am terribly excited to finally be here. As a child, I learned of the Falls that embodied the power of the element of Water, and I had always hoped to visit one day. It is my goal to gather a scant amount of water from the river and take it home to place in one of the quarters of my altar.

We quickly got the lay of the land, learning that there was an available helicopter tour, as well as a boat ride, walking tour of the tunnels, cable car ride over the whirlpool, and countless souvenir shops. Okay, just one more look over the edge – I gasp again!

Although the drop seems to go on forever, I know that it is just over 160 feet from where I am standing to the water level below. But, over one hundred thousand cubic feet of water pass over the falls every second – a gasp without looking!

Eye of the cyclops

The helicopter ride would be first – I wouldn't want to miss any part of this majestic expression of the Water element. I spot a sign for the helicopter ride. "Let's give it a whirl," I say. After paying our fare, we head to the platform where we climb into the helicopter. Up we go and firmly my hands grip the bar in front of me. I never did like heights, but I would not miss this for the world. We ride down the river, a rather simple excursion so far.

Then, rather abruptly, we find ourselves turning around and coming back the way we went. Then, hovering just briefly, we seem to plunge over the Falls. Yikes! For an instant, my inner organs seemed to all gather up around my throat for a mini-convention to discuss my obvious demise. Without remaining here very long, thank Neptune, we continue down to the whirlpool.

The whirlpool is enormous; its center reminds me of the eye of the Cyclops. Although the water appears to be moving very slowly from where we are, it is actually moving quite fast, about 30 feet per second. The river takes a rapid near 90 degree turn and we follow it from above. The subtle, soft power of nature's river turns so quickly and violently, as we see it make the turn from the whirlpool and head toward the Horseshoe Falls. Once here, our pilot descends into the center of the Horseshoe Falls – mist is rising all around us. It is so thrilling to feel air and water in harmony and such a powerful manifestation of the two.

The Maid of the Mist

What can I say about the *Maid of the Mist*? These wonderful boats, which have transported thousands of visitors throughout the past decades, travel from calm water to the rougher water beneath the Falls. Here the boat pauses for a while. Some of us are holding on to the edge of the boat as it rocks, while others are reaching for their cameras. Although the view from here is spectacular, the camera images are not very good. This is principally due to the mist that surrounds us. I decide to put the camera away and look into the mist. The faces of water nymphs are visible everywhere. I am not surprised and you wouldn't be either. There is water beneath us, splashing down all around us, and the air that we are breathing is as moist as air can be. Truly, this is one of the greatest elemental wonders of our world.

After an experience like this, I am redirected, as I find myself assessing a very different type of adventure – entering a cave in the earth to better experience the Falls. The tunnels behind the Falls are pretty well cut out and wide enough for several people to walk through. As I walk in, I can hear the roar of the Falls. I walk for some time before the air becomes very thick and damp. Now the sound is once again nearing a deafening level. I have to speak very loudly for those around to hear me. As we reach the end of the tunnel, there is truly a sight to behold – the back side of the Falls. Standing back and looking at the opening of the tunnel, as it frames the water fall, it appears as a window into another world. This is a site that I will never forget.

One final gasp before I turn around and head back to our room.

The moonbow

After dinner, we are beginning to settle down into our room for the evening. It was an exhausting day, primarily because of the emotional excitement that surged through our veins. It is also a full moon and we are beginning to feel a bit restless. "I think we should go for one final walk," I say. So, we leave our room and head toward the Falls for one last look. I am just not prepared for the breathtaking experience that I am about to have. Looking up over the falls there is a rainbow at night! The light of the full moon combines with the mist of the falls and creates a perfect rainbow.

Later the next morning, we would learn that the rainbow at night over the full moon, formed in the mist of the falls, is known locally as a moonbow. It has been a very magical night. And I suggest that if any of you can ever travel to the renowned Niagara Falls... better it be when the moon is full!

– ARMAND TABER

187

Reviews

The Book of Seshet
A Guide to the
Rosetta Tarot
http://shop.rosettatarot.com

The Rosetta Tarot, M.M. Meleen's original interpretation of the Thoth deck, and its companion guide should be considered by any reader intrigued by Crowley's vision yet confounded by its complexity. As the author acknowledges in the introduction, Crowley's *Book of Thoth* can be "difficult to digest due to…the highly esoteric nature of his thinking." *The Book of Seshet* is intended as a feminine supplement to the teachings of the Golden Dawn. It acts as a competent and graspable introduction to Crowley's deck, as well as being a charming stand-alone deck.

Several aspects of the Rosetta Tarot are remarkable: for one, the amount of artistic vigor employed to create a sense of vitality and substance within the deck's imagery is astounding. Not only is each image rendered by hand, but the media changes from suit to suit in order to best reflect each suit's inherent qualities. While many of the symbols employed in the Thoth deck can be spotted in the Rosetta cards, the deck is undoubtedly unique. The imagery is friendlier somehow, more accessible; there is an almost child-like quality to the paintings, which is not to imply amateurism, but rather unbridled enthusiasm for exploration. It is clear a substantial amount of energy has been invested in this work, and the deck becomes almost electric with the stored energy of the artist: the cards are kinetic. The deck itself is professionally printed, numbered and signed by the artist and is definitely of keepsake quality.

As for the companion booklet, though by no means exhaustive it does represent a wealth of background information helpful when approaching tarot. Not only are zodiac and Cabbalistic aspects explained, but each card is given a write up. While explanations of individual cards are detailed enough to be informative, they are not restrictive. The author recognizes tarot as a fundamentally interpretive art and so allows the reader room for intuition. Overall, the deck and booklet are highly recommended for collectors and ambitious beginners alike.

Sample spreads
The Book of Seshet concludes by offering four spreads for use with the Rosetta Tarot: two created specifically for use with the Rosetta Tarot and two spreads from the Golden Dawn tradition. The author is quick to point out that the

Rosetta Tarot is suitable for any spread, but we would like to take a moment and explore the first spread, the Rosetta Stone spread. Modeled on its namesake artifact, the Rosetta Stone spread can be used to resolve the known and unknown of a situation, explore different aspects of a relationship, as well as help decide between two options. The spread is set up in a three by three grid. The columns represent, from left to right, the past, present, and future of a situation. The rows represent, from top to bottom, the unknown (or choice two), the resolving forces, and the known (or choice one). This is modeled on the Rosetta stone, which bore Egyptian hieroglyphs at the top (an unknown language), ancient Greek script on the bottom (a known language) and Egyptian Demotic script in the middle. The presence of this third script allowed a translation to take place and thus resolve the unknown with the known. Such a sentiment seems extremely well suited to the art of tarot, which promises to make clear what meager perception has made cloudy.

Cards in the spread are laid out beginning with the known past, or bottom left hand corner of the grid. Next comes the unknown past (top left corner), and finally the resolving force of the past. Cards are laid out in this order (bottom, top, middle) in each column moving from left to right or past to future. I used this spread to inquire about a possible career switch, and the results were very pleasing. I had no trouble divining this spread (this spread and deck was also used by a friend who had no previous tarot experience and

he took to it like a fish to water!) *The Book of Seshet* clearly explained the symbolism and power encompassed in each card. For a full exploration of the Rosetta Stone spread, visit the web and see the deck in action!

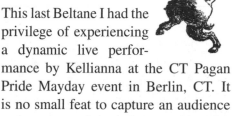

Kellianna
The Ancient Ones

This last Beltane I had the privilege of experiencing a dynamic live performance by Kellianna at the CT Pagan Pride Mayday event in Berlin, CT. It is no small feat to capture an audience and transport it to other worlds with just a guitar or simple drum along with a more than competant vocal performance. Kellianna was able to do just that with the ease that only comes from talent beyond the norm.

Kellianna's latest release *The Ancient Ones*, available on her website kellianna.com, is a delight for the Pagan heart. In the language of the early Pagan Rennaisance these tunes were called "Filk" which is a play on the concept of "Folk Music." It's been a long time since I heard "filk" done this well and I confess, I have a taste for it! The production values of *The Ancient Ones* are very high and I strongly reccomend it to our *Almanac* readership. Kellianna's first CD *Lady Moon* is also recommended.

For those who might be in a position to book acts for events, I can only say that you won't go wrong calling on Kellianna.

From a Witch's Mailbox

Home Sweet Home

I have a friend who recently moved into a new home. What would be a good gift for them?

– Cricket M.
Chicago, IL

Each culture has traditional gifts that are given for a house warming. In Hispanic culture you would give salt, rice and a broom. The salt is given so that all food is tasty, rice so that you never go hungry and a broom so that your home is always clean. In Anglo-Saxon culture you might give bread, wine, salt and a candle. Bread so that there is always food in the home, wine for joy and prosperity, salt so that your food is always tasty and a candle so that there is always light in your home.

To Charge or Not to Charge…

What do you think of Pagan Clergy charging to perform rituals and other services? Is there a standard for what is acceptable?

– Ariana V.
Facebook

As you may imagine, there is a wide range of thoughts and opinions on the subject of proper compensation for ritual services. Not every tradition or practitioner will agree on what is "acceptable." Those who don't believe in charging a monetary fee will usually accept (and usually request) some form of exchange – if not money than perhaps services rendered. For example, this past summer a ritual was performed for two dear friends; in exchange they'll be digging up a pair of rather robust hydrangea bushes from the officiant's front yard. While there is no set standard dictating payment for rituals, equitable exchanges can be agreed upon through mutual negotiation.

A Good Read

Has anyone ever written a biography on Elizabeth Pepper?

– Buddy G.
Topeka, KS

Not yet ;)

Hello, My Name is Willow

How do I meet other witches?

– Seraphina S.
Fall River, MA

Drop us a note with a description of what you are looking for and we will forward it on. You could also go to http://www.witchvox.com/. They have a myriad of listings that are sorted by geographical location. A word of caution, do your homework when checking out a new group. Of course you could always put our bumper sticker on your car. What a way to start a conversation.

Spin the Wheel

How do you pick the theme for each new issue?

– Susan A.
Facebook

To answer this question, I refer to an excerpt from our book, Witches All*:*

During the Middle Ages, when literacy began to reach all levels of society, a method of assigning a classification to each year was recorded. Its origin may have been Old Irish, although no one knows for sure. Beginning with the sign of Aries, the time of rebirth in our hemisphere, the years run in cycles of nine. Their sequence is as follows:

Sun
Moon
Earth
Fire
Air
Water
Plant
Animal
Stone

Soothsayers have used the sequence as an aid in foretelling events. Dream books, so popular in the 1930s, called it a tradition of witchcraft. Perhaps its most important function is to keep us aware of change. No year is ever quite like any other. Each brings its gifts and claims its tolls.

So year to year we pick a diverse theme that will facilitate a concentrated exploration of the natural world and our spiritual connection to it while following this sequence of nine.

A Good Listen

Where can I get some good chanting music?

– Dana M.
Ontario, CA

If you are looking for Pagan chants, a good place to start would be your local occult bookstore or one of the myriad online book stores that are out there. For those of you who use iTunes, check out the iTunes store, they have a very large selection.

Come Fly with Me

Do you know of any recipes for authentic flying ointment that has survived into the new world? Are flying ointments still in use today?

– Seth L.
Facebook

Back in the fifteenth century, flying ointments were used to aid a witch in her Sabbath flight. While the ointment may not have enabled physical flight, it certainly promoted flight of a more mental nature: the active ingredients in traditional flying ointments were toxic herbal extracts such as hemlock, belladonna and henbane. These poisons, when absorbed through the skin, caused vivid hallucinations. Indeed, a witch of olden times might indeed believe she was flying after applying this infamous ointment. Fifteenth century witches, however, were neither the first nor the only group to employ hallucinogenic substances in their rituals.

Examples can be found across the globe even today of powerful and dangerous substances being employed to open the doors of perception within a spiritual context.

No precise recipes for flying ointment have been uncovered. However, even if any authentic recipes did exist, we would be remiss to lead you to them. Their prime constituent is still, after all, poison. Even those with knowledge of the poisonous herbs in question can still become ill or die from their use.

Let us hear from you, too

We love to hear from our readers. Letters should be sent with the writer's name (or just first name or initials), address, daytime phone number and e-mail address, if available. Published material may be edited for clarity or length. All letters and e-mails will become the property of The Witches' Almanac Ltd. *and will not be returned. We regret that due to the volume of correspondence we cannot reply to all communications.*

The Witches' Almanac, Ltd.
P.O. Box 1292
Newport, RI 02840-9998
info@TheWitchesAlmanac.com
www.TheWitchesAlmanac.com

TO: The Witches' Almanac
P.O. Box 1292, Newport, RI 02840-9998
www.TheWitchesAlmanac.com

Name_____

Address_____

City_____ State_____ Zip_____

E-mail_____

WITCHCRAFT being by nature one of the secretive arts, it may not be as easy to find us next year. If you'd like to make sure we know where you are, why don't you send us your name and address? You will certainly hear from us.

News from The Witches' Almanac

Glad tidings from the staff

The Warehouse

The Witches' Almanac has moved its warehouse! Our new location allows for easier fulfillment and keeps all of our stock in one location. The fulfillment staff has worked hard at keeping this a seamless move. You won't notice a difference except that maybe your order will be filled quicker!

Storefront

Our storefront has expanded and now offers even more products in a good old fashioned brick-and-mortar location. We've also expanded our hours. Drop by and visit us in our East Greenwich, RI location. There's lots to chat about and lots of products to peruse.

The Troll Shop • 88 Main Street • East Greenwich, RI • 401-884-9800

Pagan Pride

This year's RI Pagan Pride is quickly approaching. We hope you take the time to visit us! This year's Pride is being held on August 10, 2013 at Riverside Sportsman's Association in Riverside, RI. Our booth is indoors this year, so drop by. We will be there come rain or come shine.

The Witches' Pantry

This year we have two brand new recipes to share with you. The Witches' Pantry is featuring Garlic Sauce and May Wine.

Web Extras

Did you know that some of our articles are expanded on the Web, offering even more insightful information? Find out more at www. TheWitchesAlmanac.com/AlmanacExtras.

Social Networking

Keep in touch with *The Witches' Almanac* via facebook (http://www. facebook. com/pages/The-Witches-Almanac) and twitter (http://twitter. com/#!/WitchesAlmanac).

Since 1994 Herbs & Arts has served Denver and the region,
striving to be a place of healing & sanctuary for the Pagan & Wiccan
communities, and all seekers of spiritual living.

We live with a simple intention, to put forth compassion, love & gratitude
into the universe with the belief that if we can inspire & empower healing and
spiritual connection in ourselves and others, the world will change for the better.

We make 100's of ritual oils, incenses, & bath salts for all your magickal needs.
All of our ritual products are made in sacred space and at specific lunar
& astrological times. Our webstore also has over 400 herbs, essential oils
and other items to support your connection to spirit.

Blessed be.

Herbs & Arts

www.herbsandarts.com   Denver, CO   303.388.2544

Rosarium Blends

Alchemical Concoctions to Enliven the Senses

handcrafted
Ritual Incense Blends
Enchanting Essential Oil Blends
Natural Perfumes
Erotic Apothecary

Imported
Exotic and Rare Resins
Incense Burners and Oil Diffusors
Hand Carved Wooden Altar Boxes

www.rosariumblends.com

Dikki-Jo Mullen

The Witches' Almanac Astrologer

PO Box 533024, Orlando, FL 32853
skymaiden@juno.com
http://dikkijomullen.wordpress.com

Seminars, Presentation, Convention Programs

Complete Astrology & Parapsychology Services

Paranormal Investigations

*(see the web site for astrology articles
and information about upcoming events)*

*Psychic Readings,
Reiki Healing & Spiritual Work*

Mother Mystic

401-353-3099

*Crystals • Oils
Candles • Herbs*

Open Tue – Sat 12pm to 7pm
179 Dean Street, Federal Hill
Providence, RI 02903

www.mothermystic.com

The Troll Shop

Trolls • Imports
Antiques • Collectibles

88 Main St.
East Greenwich, RI 02818
401-884-9800

☞ MARKETPLACE ☜

☞ CLASSIFIED ☜

The products and services offered above are paid advertisements.

The Witchcraft of Dame Darrel of York

Charles Godfrey Leland

Introduction by Robert Mathiesen

The Witches' Almanac presents:

- *A previously unpublished work by folklorist Charles Godfrey Leland.*
- *Published in full color facsimile with a text transcript.*
- *Forward by Prof. Robert Mathiesen.*

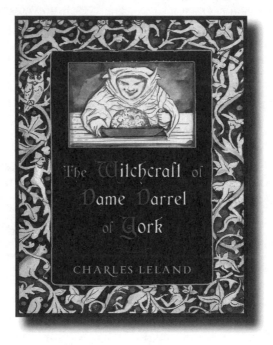

This beautifully reproduced facsimile of the illuminated manuscript will shed light on an ancient tradition as well as provide the basis for a modern practice. It will be treasured by those practicing Pagans, scholars, and all those fascinated by the legend and lore of England.

Standard hardcover edition ($65.00).
Deluxe numbered edition with slipcase ($85.00).
Exclusive full leather bound, numbered and slip cased edition ($145.00).

For further information visit http://TheWitchesAlmanac.com/damedarrel.html

ARADIA
GOSPEL OF THE WITCHES
Charles Godfrey Leland

ARADIA IS THE FIRST work in English in which witchcraft is portrayed as an underground old religion, surviving in secret from ancient pagan times.

- Used as a core text by many modern neo-pagans.
- Foundation material containing traditional witchcraft practices
- This special edition features appreciations by such authors and luminaries as Paul Huson, Raven Grimassi, Judika Illes, Michael Howard, Christopher Penczak, Myth Woodling, Christina Oakley Harrington, Patricia Della-Piana, Jimahl di Fiosa and Donald Weiser. A beautiful and compelling work, this edition has brought the format up to date, while keeping the text unchanged. 172 pages $16.95

❧ *Newly expanded classics!* ☙

The ABC of Magic Charms
Elizabeth Pepper

SINCE THE DAWN of mankind, an obscure instinct in the human spirit has sought protection from mysterious forces beyond mortal control. Human beings sought benefaction in the three realms that share Earth with us — animal, mineral, vegetable. All three, humanity discovered, contain mysterious properties discovered over millennia through occult divination. An enlarged edition of *Magic Charms from A to Z*, compiled by the staff of *The Witches' Almanac.* $12.95

The Little Book of Magical Creatures
Elizabeth Pepper and Barbara Stacy

A loving tribute to the animal kingdom

AN UPDATE of the classic *Magical Creatures*, featuring Animals Tame, Animals Wild, Animals Fabulous – plus an added section of enchanting animal myths from other times, other places. *A must for all animal lovers.* $12.95

✤ a lady shape-shifts into a white doe ✤ two bears soar skyward
✤ Brian Boru rides a wild horse ✤ a wolf growls dire prophecy

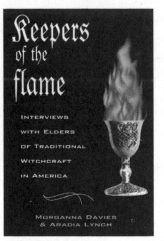

A Treasury from past editions...

Perfect for study or casual reading, Witches All *is a collection from* The Witches' Almanac *publications of the past. Arranged by topics, the book, like the popular almanacs, is thought provoking and often spurs me on to a tangent leading to even greater discovery. The information and art in the book – astrological attributes, spells, recipes, history, facts & figures is a great reminder of the history of the Craft, not just in recent years, but in the early days of the Witchcraft Revival in this century: the witch in an historical and cultural perspective.* Ty Bevington, Circle of the Wicker Man, Columbus, Ohio

Absolutely beautiful! I recently ordered Witches All *and I have to say I wasn't disappointed. The artwork and articles are first rate and for a longtime* Witches' Almanac *fan, it is a wonderful addition to my collection.* Witches' Almanac *devotees and newbies alike will love this latest effort. Very worth getting.*
Tarot3, Willits, California

GREEK GODS IN LOVE

Barbara Stacy casts a marvelously original eye on the beloved stories of Greek deities, replete with amorous oddities and escapades. We relish these tales in all their splendor and antic humor, and offer an inspired storyteller's fresh version of the old, old mythical magic.

MAGIC CHARMS FROM A TO Z

A treasury of amulets, talismans, fetishes and other lucky objects compiled by the staff of *The Witches' Almanac*. An invaluable guide for all who respond to the call of mystery and enchantment.

LOVE CHARMS

Love has many forms, many aspects. Ceremonies performed in witchcraft celebrate the joy and the blessings of love. Here is a collection of love charms to use now and ever after.

MAGICAL CREATURES

Mystic tradition grants pride of place to many members of the animal kingdom. Some share our life. Others live wild and free. Still others never lived at all, springing instead from the remarkable power of human imagination.

ANCIENT ROMAN HOLIDAYS

The glory that was Rome awaits you in Barbara Stacy's classic presentation of a festive year in pagan times. Here are the gods and goddesses as the Romans conceived them, accompanied by the annual rites performed in their worship. Scholarly, light-hearted – a rare combination.

CELTIC TREE MAGIC

Robert Graves in *The White Goddess* writes of the significance of trees in the old Celtic lore. *Celtic Tree Magic* is an investigation of the sacred trees in the remarkable Beth-Luis-Nion alphabet; their role in folklore, poetry, and mysticism.

MOON LORE

As both the largest and the brightest object in the night sky, and the only one to appear in phases, the Moon has been a rich source of myth for as long as there have been mythmakers.

MAGIC SPELLS AND INCANTATIONS

Words have magic power. Their sound, spoken or sung, has ever been a part of mystic ritual. From ancient Egypt to the present, those who practice the art of enchantment have drawn inspiration from a treasury of thoughts and themes passed down through the ages.

LOVE FEASTS

Creating meals to share with the one you love can be a sacred ceremony in itself. With the witch in mind, culinary adept Christine Fox offers magical menus and recipes for every month in the year.

RANDOM RECOLLECTIONS
II, III, IV

Pages culled from the original (no longer available) issues of *The Witches' Almanac*, published annually throughout the 1970's, are now available in a series of tasteful booklets. A treasure for those who missed us the first time around; keepsakes for those who remember.

Order Form

Each timeless edition of *The Witches' Almanac* is unique.
Limited numbers of previous years' editions are available.

Item	Price	Qty.	Total
2014-2015 The Witches' Almanac	$12.95		
2013-2014 The Witches' Almanac	$11.95		
2012-2013 The Witches' Almanac	$11.95		
2011-2012 The Witches' Almanac	$11.95		
2010-2011 The Witches' Almanac	$11.95		
2009-2010 The Witches' Almanac	$11.95		
2008-2009 The Witches' Almanac	$10.95		
2007-2008 The Witches' Almanac	$9.95		
2006-2007 The Witches' Almanac	$8.95		
2005-2006 The Witches' Almanac	$8.95		
2004-2005 The Witches' Almanac	$8.95		
2003-2004 The Witches' Almanac	$8.95		
2002-2003 The Witches' Almanac	$7.95		
2001-2002 The Witches' Almanac	$7.95		
2000-2001 The Witches' Almanac	$7.95		
1999-2000 The Witches' Almanac	$7.95		
1998-1999 The Witches' Almanac	$6.95		
1997-1998 The Witches' Almanac	$6.95		
1996-1997 The Witches' Almanac	$6.95		
1995-1996 The Witches' Almanac	$6.95		
1994-1995 The Witches' Almanac	$5.95		
1993-1994 The Witches' Almanac	$5.95		
The Witchcraft of Dame Darrel of York, clothbound	$65.00		
Aradia or The Gospel of the Witches	$16.95		
The Horned Shepherd	$16.95		
The ABC of Magic Charms	$12.95		
The Little Book of Magical Creatures	$12.95		
Greek Gods in Love	$15.95		
Witches All	$13.95		
Ancient Roman Holidays	$6.95		
Celtic Tree Magic	$7.95		
Love Charms	$6.95		
Love Feasts	$6.95		
Magic Charms from A to Z	$12.95		
Magical Creatures	$12.95		
Magic Spells and Incantations	$12.95		
Moon Lore	$7.95		
Random Recollections II, III or IV (circle your choices)	$3.95		
SALE 20 back issues with free book bag and free shipping	$100.00		
The Rede of the Wiccae	$22.95		
Keepers of the Flame	$20.95		
Subtotal			
Tax (7% sales tax for RI customers)			
Shipping & Handling (*See shipping rates section*)			
TOTAL			

BRACELETS			
Item	**Price**	**Qty.**	**Total**
Agate, Green	$5.95		
Agate, Moss	$5.95		
Agate, Natural	$5.95		
Agate, Red	$5.95		
Amethyst	$5.95		
Aventurine	$5.95		
Fluorite	$5.95		
Jade, African	$5.95		
Jade, White	$5.95		
Jasper, Picture	$5.95		
Jasper, Red	$5.95		
Lapis Lazuli	$5.95		
Malachite	$5.95		
Moonstone	$5.95		
Obsidian	$5.95		
Onyx, Black	$5.95		
Opal	$5.95		
Quartz Crystal	$5.95		
Quartz, Rose	$5.95		
Rhodonite	$5.95		
Sodalite	$5.95		
Tigereye	$5.95		
Turquoise	$5.95		
Unakite	$5.95		
Subtotal			
Tax (7% for RI customers)			
Shipping & Handling (*See shipping rates section*)			
TOTAL			

MISCELLANY			
Item	**Price**	**Qty.**	**Total**
Pouch	$3.95		
Matches: *10 small individual boxes*	$5.00		
Matches: *1 large box of 50 individual boxes*	$20.00		
Natural/Black Book Bag	$17.95		
Red/Black Book Bag	$17.95		
Hooded Sweatshirt, Blk	$30.00		
Hooded Sweatshirt, Red	$30.00		
L-Sleeve T, Black	$20.00		
L-Sleeve T, Red	$20.00		
S-Sleeve T, Black/W	$15.00		
S-Sleeve T, Black/R	$15.00		
S-Sleeve T, Dk H/R	$15.00		
S-Sleeve T, Dk H/W	$15.00		
S-Sleeve T, Red/B	$15.00		
S-Sleeve T, Ash/R	$15.00		
S-Sleeve T, Purple/W	$15.00		
Postcards – set of 12	$3.00		
Bookmarks – set of 12	$1.00		
Magnets – set of 3	$1.50		
Promo Pack	$7.00		
Subtotal			
Tax (7% sales tax for RI customers)			
Shipping & Handling (*See shipping rates section*)			
TOTAL			

SHIPPING & HANDLING CHARGES

BOOKS: One book, add $4.00. Each additional book add $1.50

POUCH: One pouch, $2.00. Each additional pouch add $1.50

MATCHES: Ten individual boxes, add $2.50.
One large box of fifty, add $6.00. Each additional large box add $3.50.

BOOKBAGS: $4.00 per bookbag.

BRACELETS: $2.00 per bracelet.

Send a check or money order payable in U. S. funds or credit card details to:

The Witches' Almanac, Ltd., PO Box 1292, Newport, RI 02840-9998

(401) 847-3388 (phone) • (888) 897-3388 (fax)
Email: info@TheWitchesAlmanac.com • www.TheWitchesAlmanac.com